Business Writing

with

Style

Strategies
for Success

John Tarrant

JOHN WILEY & SONS, INC.

New York, Chichester, Brisbane, Toronto, Singapore

To Dot

Library of Congress Cataloging-in-Publication Data

Tarrant, John J.
    Business writing with style : strategies for success /
    by John Tarrant.
        p.   cm.
    Includes bibliographical references.
    ISBN 0–471–53211–8. — ISBN 0–471–53212–6 (pbk.)
    1. Business writing.   I. Title.
    HF5718.3.T37   1991
    808′.06665—dc20   90–24548

Printed in the United States of America

91 92 10 9 8 7 6 5 4 3 2 1

Preface

Warning! *This book may shock you.*

If you're expecting a conventional primer on writing, with rules of grammar and instructions on how to diagram a sentence, you won't find it in these pages.

If you want another book that rehashes the schoolroom staples of formal outlining and slavish rewriting, you'll be disappointed.

And if you're looking forward to being told when it's proper to use a comma or a semicolon, it's only fair to prepare you for a blow.

This is a book of *advanced writing techniques for business.* It's written for gifted people who want to write as well as they speak.

Yes, you'll find a section on rules of writing—but that section tells you when to break the rules as well as when to follow them.

Formal outlining takes too long for busy people. Instead, this book gives you a commonsense Q&A method of instant organization of business documents.

Routine revision drains away color and spontaneity. Here you'll find unconventional approaches that help you to get it right the first time.

Above all, this book is a *catalog of stylistic strategies* designed to make your business writing impressive *and* effective. With these strategies you can achieve personal objectives along with the more obvious job-related objectives of business writing. How many writing texts give you a section on office politics and dirty tricks?

When your writing skill matches your other skills, you can accomplish more—and have fun doing it!

Acknowledgments

Thanks—to Fritz Jellinghaus, Paul Fargis, Mort Feinberg, and Ed Halloran for good suggestions . . . to Pat Tarrant, John Lytle, and Peggy Tarrant for guidance, analysis, and excellent examples of business writing . . . to Mike Hamilton for strong, perceptive editorial support . . . to the organizations and people who made documents and resources available to me . . . and to Dorothy Tarrant, beloved comrade and professional partner.

Contents

CHAPTER 1

Better Writing Can Pay Big Dividends

B usiness *talk* is rich and varied, a wellspring of vitality and change in the language. Business people make up new verbs, draw wild analogies, paint vivid word pictures—when they are speaking.

Business *writing* is dull. Managers who talk fluently write constrictedly. Speech sparkles; memos mumble. You read the stuff on the page or the screen dutifully, because you have to. But how often are you jolted by business documents—or intrigued, or moved, or inspired, or persuaded?

When we talk, we feel free to use figures of speech that we would never use in writing, because writing requires more formality. A sales manager writes, "I feel he is somewhat lacking in basic marketing skills," In person, the manager says, "He couldn't sell beer on a troopship."

Obviously there are differences. Writing isn't just talking in print. But writing, like talking, can be colorful, interesting, riveting.

Why isn't business writing as resourceful and effective as business talking? One reason is that an amazing number of managers *don't try* to write better. They strive for excellence in other areas, but they settle for mediocrity in writing.

If you want to write better, you can. The first step is to realize that good writing can be learned and developed.

Good writing is fun. You thrill when the right word clicks into place. You stand taller because you have mastered the essential craft of written communication. You feel good because you *are* good at something that is important, demanding, and worth being good at.

Bad writing used to be the dirty underwear of the executive. It could be hidden. A literate (and underpaid) secretary took the boss's dictated ramblings and turned them into decent prose. Even without the secretary-ghostwriter, the poor writer could get by. Writing was not all that important. You talked to people, called them on the phone. Persuasion took place belly to belly, not by remote control.

Good Writing as a Superconductor

Writing should act as a superconductor. The superconductor is a medium through which electricity moves without interference, diffusion, or distortion. The initial impulse emerges as the final impulse, at nearly the speed of light.

When you have developed a fluent writing style it acts as a superconductor, conveying all your fire, subtlety, and strength exactly as you intend it. You can use language to inform, inspire, probe, analyze—all the things managers are taught to do.

You can (as you will find out in the following pages) also use language to cover your rear, impress your bosses, confound your rivals, improve your image—all the things you have to do to survive and win in the corporate career jungle.

What You Learned in School: Bad Writing

Teachers discourage good writing. They hand out ''teaching materials'' that are written atrociously. They talk about the importance of ''communications skills'' while skimping on useful writing instruction.

Why? Well, if you're a mediocre writer, it's easy to decide that good writing isn't important. And most teachers—including instructors at graduate business schools—are not good writers. Their skills have rusted in the swamps of academia. And they were probably not so hot to start with. Writing ability has not been a key criterion in deciding who climbs to the top of the greasy academic pole.

So the business training you receive doesn't help you to write better. It straps you into a straitjacket. Your natural instinct for lively writing is tied up with dreary rules about how you must make outlines (with capital letters and small letters, Arabic numerals and Roman numerals) and how you must do first drafts, second drafts, drafts ad infinitum.

Rules are not writing. Rules impose a formal predictability on writing. One of the critical objectives of this book is to free you from straitjacketing rules. You *don't* have to make formal outlines. You *don't* have to write a first draft and then a second draft. In fact, these slavish practices take the freshness out of your writing.

This is a book about *possibilities* and *promise*. If you have the brains to be a good manager, you have the potential skill to write well.

Managing across Thousands of Miles

Today we do business by remote control. Managers reach out through networks—sometimes to the other side of the world—to instruct, motivate, analyze, confer, criticize. You have to be able to communicate effectively with people who are far away.

You do this by phone. And you do it by writing.

So writing skill is more important than ever before. In two ways. You need good writing to do your job well. And you need good writing to present yourself favorably to those whose decisions will affect your career. Your image is on the line with people who judge you—to a considerable degree—on the basis of your writing.

Writing Moves to Center Stage

Writing skill has become an important management tool. This is a fairly recent development. Not long ago writing was a fringe attribute—great if you could do it, but not considered essential to success. Today, writing is regarded as essential. Merit reviews assess progress in this area. Once it would have seemed strange for a senior manager to comment, ''She's a good writer,'' or, ''His writing still needs work.'' These days you expect to see writing evaluated in performance appraisals. (And, as a corollary, senior managers are going to have to find ways to help their people write better.)

Writing-Starved Business Graduates

Management teaching has not caught up with the growing importance of writing. Corporate leaders, educators, and training directors lament the situation. Typically, *Training & Development Journal* (April 1990) says:

Newly graduated business majors with solid academic preparation in business are frequently incapable of communicating effectively, especially when the communication must be in writing. . . . Business schools tend to emphasize quantitative skills—they relegate writing to required composition classes or require students to write without giving them adequate instruction.

Most Writing Instruction Books Don't Work

You're bright, energetic, ambitious, firmly embarked on your career. You talk confidently and fluently. You know the meanings of words and the basics of grammar. You have a good grasp of the tools or management, and you're using them better as you gain experience.

But you're concerned about your writing. You know writing is important. You try hard—within the limits of time pressure—to compose good documents, but in spite of your efforts they come out stiff or simplistic. Your writing doesn't reflect your personality or your ability.

So you look for help. You take a course, or you get a book on business writing. You're conscientious in doing your lessons.

That's just the trouble. Most writing instruction for managers is "doing your lessons." There's a depressing "back-to-school" air about it. As a kid you were bored with all the stuff about predicates and gerunds and participles. You trudged unenthusiastically through the task of making an outline. You rebelled at the constant necessity to revise.

You still dislike formal outlining, editing, and revision. You may acknowledge that it's necessary and try to go through the prescribed steps to produce a document, but it takes a lot of time, and it's certainly not fun.

Worst of all, the schoolbook approach doesn't seem to help your writing. By the time you've finished building a painstaking outline, composing a first draft, editing, and finishing a second draft, the juice is all squeezed out of your message. It's stiff and cumbersome.

Maybe all this drudgery would be worth it if the result were a document that gets the job done. But unfortunately the product is apt to be just as boring to read as it was to write.

Racing against Time

There's another factor that makes the conventional approach inadequate for today's business writing—*time*. We work over great distances today—and we work instantaneously. The velocity of communication has increased with headlong speed. Within the memory of living people, the standard method of sending written communication was first-class mail, which traveled by train. When you really had to get it there fast, you sent it airmail. Then all first-class mail became airmail. This was found to be inadequate. Overnight became the norm. Expressing (or "Fedexing") something was now standard. Ordinary mail became the way of sending material so unimportant as to be one step removed from the wastebasket.

Now we have fax, E-mail, and the whole constellation of instantaneous transmission media. Overnight is slow. And the heightened speed of transmission imposes a corresponding rush on the task of composition. Few managers enjoy the luxury of being able to do an outline, a first draft, and as many subsequent drafts as it takes to do the trick.

Time was that managers were supported by secretaries (later executive secretaries or executive assistants) who would take a dictated jumble of ideas and create a crisp letter or memo. Some of the business world's most successful leaders were so bad at writing that they would have seemed virtually illiterate—if anyone had ever seen what they wrote. They enjoyed the services of people who made them look good on paper.

That's going out of style. And a good thing, too. Managers should not be written for. They should *write*.

The Need for Speed

You can't afford the time to plod through the conventional method of writing a business document. Besides, it bores you. And the process curdles your words into stiffness and dullness.

Modern business demands a new approach, one that telescopes the process and pumps vitality into the finished product. Today's business writer has to find a way to *write well the first time,* without formal outlining and first-drafting.

Playing It Safe and "Writing Fat"

Until recently, executives at one large insurance company went to extremes in caution in their writing. When composing memos on, let's say, the dissemination of certain underwriting data, instead of expressing their own thoughts in their own words, these executives would rummage around in the files for old memos written on the same subject—preferably memos written by authority figures like board chairmen and CEOs. The authors would then lift "safe terms" from these old documents and incorporate them into their current work.

We can all agree that this is ludicrous. But a lot of executives play it safe when they write. One way they do this is by using more words than are needed to make the point:

> The purpose of this document is to establish and describe the position of Argentina Country Director (ACD), together with a listing of the functions that guide the activities of this position, and a description of the organizational structure within which the parameters of the position will be carried out.

This opening paragraph is followed by nine pages of material on job responsibilities, reporting relationships, and staffing requirements. The paragraph could have been shortened to this:

This document describes the position of Argentina Country Director (ACD).

In fact you could do the job with just a title:

ARGENTINA COUNTRY DIRECTOR: A NEW POSITION

The writer of the original paragraph used so many words because he had been criticized repeatedly for lack of "comprehensiveness" in previous documents. He was being hypercautious; his big motivation was not to be criticized again for the same shortcoming.

Some bosses never commend brevity, but always pounce when they think something's been handled at insufficient length. This attitude fosters wordiness.

Lawyers are notorious for using a lot of words where one would do:

... including, without limiting the generality of the foregoing, the names of any of its customers, the prices it obtains or has obtained or at which it sells or has sold its products, or any other information of, about, or concerning the business of the Company, its manner of operation, its plans, processes, or other data of any kind, nature or description without regard to whether any or all of the foregoing matters would be deemed confidential, material, or important . . .

This passage (from *Perks and Parachutes* by John Tarrant, Simon & Schuster, 1985, p. 220) may look like a parody, but it is an actual (and not untypical) quote from an employment contract. The lawyer who wrote this was not aiming for stylishness. When pressed, lawyers will confess that they use all those extra words because, in a lawsuit, each word might be considered to have a slightly different shade of meaning. The use of one word would speed up the document but might give your opponent a loophole.

This rationale for wordiness may not be elegant (or even valid), but at least it's a rationale. In most cases, there's no credible reason for managers to do the same thing when writing business documents.

Consider your own writing. Do you "write fat"? If so, do you do it because you're writing scared? Because you've been criticized for not writing enough words? It's one thing to skimp on coverage of an important topic, or to omit it altogether. It's quite another thing to have your paragraphs evaluated by the pound. Find out. Talk to the person who criticized your writing. Make sure that your documents contain all that they need to contain. Then work on conveying that content in the most effective style, without excess verbiage.

Copycatting is another reason for obese writing. New managers see the way it's been done before, and they copy it. You may be doing that, consciously or unconsciously. If this is the case, even to some extent, you're performing at less than your best because of precedent. Do you do that in other areas of the job? You're probably getting paid to do your best in all phases of the game: to do your own thinking, to look for the most effective approaches without regard to precedent, to be innovative. It's sad when innovative thinking is conveyed in shopworn language because the writer did it the way it had been done in the past.

When wordiness is the norm, a manager can achieve quite a striking effect through brevity. Bosses may not applaud the style specifically, but they may well be impressed with the writer's incisiveness and strength.

If you're "writing fat" because you want to play it safe or because others write that way, it's time to stop. Generalized fear or vague precedent are not good enough reasons to use too many words. Your thoughts, if they are worthy at all, deserve better.

Occasionally there may be reasons for wordiness. As we discuss elsewhere in this book, there are times when you may be writing deliberately to slow things up for strategic reasons. Or it may be that one of your bosses is unshakably opposed to brevity, for whatever reason. If it's necessary to put in excess verbiage, do so. But have a good reason. Understand that it's an aberration. And don't let yourself drift into the habit.

In general, however, bad writing is not really "playing it safe." You are failing to dress your ideas for success. Instead, you're clothing them in the drab and suffocating garments of mediocrity. And you are missing the chance to have an impact on people who are forming their impressions about you, at least in part, by what you write. Verbal obesity is not a component of promotability.

WriTalk—The New Communication

Computer networks are changing the ways in which we "talk" with each other. Millions of people "talk" with each other through images on screens. Now that fax is being combined with the computer, we send short messages or documents hundreds of pages long . . . to one addressee or thousands . . . next door or halfway around the world.

Networks like CompuServe are big and getting bigger. Larger companies have their own networks. The computer connection is rapidly becoming a dominant method of business communication.

This new form of communication is creating new styles and new approaches to using words. Once you had, basically, two communications choices. If you wanted instant, personal contact with somebody some distance away, you picked up the phone. If it wasn't necessary to do it by phone, you put it in the mail. Federal Express and other fast carriers have assumed a key role in exchanging documents, but they are still mail services.

Now we exchange words by wire. It's faster than the fastest mail—sometimes virtually instantaneous. But it does not have the immediacy and spontaneity of telephone talk. This communications form is a hybrid—composed and received in the form of print, but having many of the aspects of direct speech. We might call it WriTalk.

WriTalk calls for a new approach to composition. The formality (often shading toward stiffness) of traditional business letters and memos just does not work on the CRT. You need to be "looser" and "tighter" at the same time. *Looser* in the sense that the "talk" aspect of this communications form requires flexibility and immediacy. *Tighter* in the sense that the nature of the screen calls for shorter blocks of copy and a stronger narrative thread.

Those who master WriTalk will have a distinct advantage over those who don't. Managers who remain chained to the traditional approach—formal outlines, painstaking revisions, conventional formats—will find themselves fighting the medium rather than taking advantage of it.

The fact is that *speed is essential* in written business communications today. The computer network is just one major factor in the greater importance of writing quickly and well. In every aspect of business, people are under tremendous pressure to *get it done now*. Managers no longer have the leisure to sit around composing documents. People no longer have the time or the patience to read wasted words or stilted paragraphs.

A New Way of Writing

This book gives you a way of writing that meets the new urgencies of business. When you're free of some of the formalistic burdens of the past, when you write freely and expressively rather than dutifully and defensively, you possess a remarkable gift—the ability to convey thought and feeling as well as information via the printed word.

You'll profit from the gift—and you'll enjoy it.

Word Processing Is Not Thought Processing

The methods presented in this book apply to writing via computer as well as by other means. Word-processing technology makes it easy to change words and to move paragraphs around. The computer is a blessing to business writers—but not an unmixed blessing. One problem is that writers may fall victim to the "pinball effect." They give in to the temptation to twiddle. Moving words does not, in itself, create a stronger document. The important thing is to have a procedure that ensures that every change is a change for the better— and that helps you to progress toward the point at which you're free from the need to make formal outlines and first drafts.

The greatest benefit of the word processor is that, when you have mastered it to the degree that its use becomes automatic, you are better able to think while you write and to apply your thinking to systematic improvement of the written product.

Think before processing. Popping words around on a screen is not revision.

CHAPTER 2

Write-Prep: How to Get Organized

Aim for Your Primary Target

G*et ready to write by spending a couple of minutes thinking about your reader or readers.*

This seems like an obvious step. However, it's often skipped. The writer embarks on the document without considering the readers and without asking how those readers are likely to respond.

So, as you start to create your document, run down this list of questions.

Reader-Evaluation Workout

To whom are you writing? One person? Several?
If several, is there one major target?
What's the target person like?
    Analytical?
    Impulsive? Deliberate?
    Decisive? Indecisive?
    Sense of humor?
    Narrowly focused? Wide-ranging?
    Experienced? New in the job?
    Ambitious?
    Secure? Insecure?
    Tense? Relaxed?

Now let's move on to questions involving the relationship between you and your primary targets.

Obviously a paramount consideration is the organization chart—are you writing to superiors, equals, subordinates? Move beyond these main considerations to other aspects of the relationship:

Friendly?
Touchy?
Does the person like you? Respect you? Trust you? Resent you? Fear you?
Do you see each other often? Seldom?
Do you usually agree? Often disagree?

To some degree your document should be shaped by the relationship. For example, if you're on cordial terms, you may feel free to be blunt in disagreement. If the relationship is strained, you may want to state your disagreement in softer terms (not primarily because you're worried about hurting the other guy's feelings, but because you make your point better if it's received with a minimum of resentment).

Form as clear a mental picture as you can of the person you're writing to. With that target before you, you're ready to move on to the job of organizing the document.

Ancillary Targets

Frequently your document will go beyond your primary targets, to FYI addressees—managers up the chain of command, counterparts in other divisions, staff people in human resources, corporate planning, etc. You're not writing to have a direct effect on these folks. However, they're reading your words and, through those words, forming or modifying an impression of you.

Think about the most influential of these ancillary targets. You're not going to shape your document solely to make yourself more attractive or interesting to these people. But it's a consideration. Let's say, for example, that you know the chairman of the board hates appendixes; he prefers all the material to be incorporated into the main body of the text. Well, forearmed with this knowledge, it makes sense to accommodate the inclinations of the chairman, even though he's not the action addressee.

Culture and Context

Every organization has its own culture. When you're a part of the organization—and have been for some time—it's hard to see it that way. Fish don't think about the chemical components of the water they swim in.

Culture affects the way we work in groups, so it's extremely worthwhile to think about the topic now and then. Culture is relevant to your writing. The context within which your words are read is shaped by various factors—the topics, the author, the time frame, the nature of the company, etc. It's also shaped by that intangible, but not unimportant, entity, the organizational culture. And the culture affects the way things are written.

For example, the "Procter memo" used to be a standard model for organizing a business document. This format was developed quite a while ago at Procter & Gamble—a sober, painstaking, methodical consumer goods company that favored a highly structured organization: statement of the topic, background, factors, recommendations, etc. The advertising agencies working with Procter—and there are a great many—tended to adopt the Procter format for *all* their communications.

This didn't always make sense. The Procter format suits the Procter culture. But most ad agencies have a looser, more free-swinging culture, which should be reflected in their written communications. It's logical (not to say mandatory) for account executives to use the Procter structure when communicating with that client. The trouble is that some Procter agencies try to use this buttoned-up approach in all their documents. The format simply does not suit the culture of the organization. Creative types sneer at it. And more informal client companies start to think of the agency as hidebound and stuffy when they keep getting these elaborately formal memos.

How is the culture of your organization reflected in written documents? Do they tend to be uniform or varied? Long or short? Blunt or diplomatic? Tightly focused or wide-ranging?

It helps to be aware of the context within which you're writing. Say, for example, certain kinds of memos always start with the posing of a question, then discuss the factors, and finally wind up with a recommendation. People who are used to this organization will be somewhat surprised to run across anything different.

Now you're about to write that kind of memo. You can follow the customary format—or you can pitch a change of pace, moving the recommendations up front.

There are advantages in either approach, depending on the circumstances. if what you're writing is a routine document, without any particular novelty or tremendous significance, then you're probably well advised to do it the way it's usually done. If, however, you feel you have an unusual message, deserving of special attention, change the format. You'll probably attract more attention, if only to a small degree. And you'll be separating yourself from the herd, in format as well as in content.

But you have to know the cultural context before you can decide whether to depart from it.

Getting Ready to Write

Here are some other questions to consider:

What else has been written on this topic?

How recently has it been covered? Does the addressee know all about it? Or need to be reminded?

Has any aspect been misinterpreted? Ignored? Given insufficient attention? Too much attention?

What is the most important new insight you can contribute?

Are you unsure about any element of what you're going to say? Can the weakness be repaired by more research? Should your document wait?

How do you want your reader to react?

What are the biggest obstacles to obtaining the desired reaction? Prejudice? Is your reader neutral? Favorable? Unfavorable?

Is the reader well versed in the subject?

Is the topic your own ''turf,'' the other guy's turf, everybody's turf?

By sitting down and thinking about relevant questions you can free yourself from the chore of making a formal outline. And you'll be launched on the creation of a more effective document.

Now let's proceed to *structure*. Again, we'll use the question-and-answer technique.

An Easy Way to Outline Anything

''First make an outline.'' Dismal words. A boring chore. But without an outline, how can you organize your document?

Think of the outline as a series of questions. Every part of the document should answer a logical question. Put yourself in the shoes of the most important person who will be reading what you write. Jot down the questions that person is entitled to ask. Put the questions in logical order.

And there's your outline!

To get you started, here are sample question-method outlines for twenty-three standard situations.

Making a Presentation

1. What is this about?
2. Why should I pay attention to it?

3. What's the objective?
4. How will the objective be achieved?
5. What will it cost?
6. How long will it take?
7. What are the risks?
8. What's the potential payoff?
9. What's the next step?

Instructing a Subordinate

1. Why is this important?
2. What has to be done?
3. What's the time frame?
4. How will progress be measured?
5. What help will I get?
6. Will I be recognized for doing a good job?

Conveying Information

1. What's this about?
2. What does it mean to me?
3. What are the details?
4. Which parts are most important?
5. What am I supposed to do about it?
6. How do I start?

Making a Recommendation

1. What's the topic?
2. What do you recommend?
3. On what do you base your recommendation?
4. How strongly do you feel about it?
5. Do you want reactions?
6. What's the next step?

Persuading Someone Who Is Leaning the Other Way

1. Why should I listen to your argument?
2. Do you understand my position?
3. What's in this for you?
4. What are the elements of your case?
5. What happens if I buy your argument?

Giving a Reaction

1. How do I feel about this?
2. Have I really considered all the points?
3. How will my reaction affect the project?

4. What are the reasons for my reaction?
5. Am I open to argument?

Selling Through a Third Party

1. What are the benefits of your propositions?
2. If I recommend it, what's in it for me?
3. How can I be sure I won't look bad?
4. What should I say in pushing the idea?

Circulating Documents—Covering Memo

1. What's this about?
2. Why am I supposed to look at it?
3. Which particular parts should I look at?
4. How does this material relate to my job?
5. What follow-up, if any, is required of me?

Putting on the Pressure for Payment or Performance

1. What am I supposed to do?
2. How much does the writer know about the commitment I made?
3. What happens if I do nothing?
4. Can I satisfy part of the commitment?
5. If so, how much do I have to pay or do?
6. How much time do I have?
7. How much do I have to fear if I don't come through?
8. Is the writer tough enough to make good on the threat?

Making an Interim Report

1. What's this about?
2. Is the project on track?
3. What problems is the writer running into?
4. Anything for me to worry about?
5. Any action required of me?

Selling an Idea

1. What's the area?
2. What is the problem to be solved?
3. What is the opportunity if the problem is solved?
4. What is your idea?
5. Why will it work?
6. Has it been tried elsewhere?
7. Why is your idea the best possible course?
8. Who else endorses your idea?

9. What will it cost?
10. What's the timetable?
11. What's the first step?

Announcing a Change

1. What is the change?
2. Why is it being made?
3. How will it affect the project or work situation?
4. How will it affect the individuals involved?
5. When should the change be made?
6. Who is responsible for making the change?
7. Are any other changes likely?

Announcing a New Employee

1. Who is the person?
2. What's the job?
3. How will the new employee interact with others?
4. Why is the new employee a good addition?

Making a Request

1. What do you want?
2. Why do you want it?
3. What's in it for the person granting the request?
4. What may you do in return?
5. What's the first step if the request is granted?

Registering Disagreement

1. What's the topic?
2. What do you disagree with? (Some, all?)
3. Why do you disagree?
4. What do you think will happen if you are not heeded?
5. Do you have evidence to support your position?
6. What alternative do you suggest?

Firming Up Support for a Course of Action

1. Are you grateful for the support?
2. Who else is on board?
3. What would you like the supporter to do first?
4. How will the support benefit the addressee?
5. What's going to happen next?

Criticism

1. What is your criticism?
2. How serious is it?

3. How do you support and document your criticism?
4. What should the reader do to straighten things out?
5. Are you available for discussion?
6. What help will you provide?
7. What goals and subgoals would you establish?
8. What's the next step?

Briefing a New Boss

1. Who are you?
2. What are you working on?
3. How important is it?
4. What's been done?
5. What remains to be done?
6. Is it under control?
7. What can the boss expect to hear from you next?

Briefing a New Subordinate

1. What's the project?
2. What stage is it at?
3. Who else is working on it?
4. Are there any changes required?
5. What should the subordinate do?
6. What help is available?
7. When does it have to be done?
8. How do you want to be informed about it?

Setting Up a Meeting

1. What is the meeting about?
2. What is the relative importance of the agenda items?
3. Where and when?
4. Who should attend?
5. Any special preparation by attendees?
6. Who will run the meeting?
7. How long will it last?

Making a Full-Scale Report

1. What is it about?
2. What is the objective?
3. What has been done to achieve the objective?
4. How well has it worked?
5. What problems remain?
6. What's going to happen next?

7. Are there contingency plans?
8. What is the timetable?
9. What should be done now?

Inquiry—Finding Out the Facts

1. What do you want to know?
2. Why do you want to know it?
3. How much do you already know?
4. How urgent is the answer?
5. What will you do if you don't get the information?

Getting Cooperation

1. How important is it?
2. What are you doing to make the project go?
3. What do your readers get out of cooperating?
4. Exactly what form should cooperation take?
5. Will you do anything in return?
6. What's the first thing you'd like done?

Leading Questions

How do you attract the reader's interest in a subject that has been covered over and over again?

Use a change of pace. One possibility: make your lead sentence a question. Here's a lead that dutifully covers the ground:

This report evaluates various factors in the market resistance to our canine nutrition products.

Eyes glaze over. Not that the topic is not important. It's vital. But the reader has heard it all before.

Try a question:

Why don't dogs like our dog food?

It's simple. It says what the memo is about. It sets a down-to-earth tone of vigorous inquiry. And it's different.

More Leading Questions

The *question method* is a good way of structuring a document. You deploy logical questions in logical order, answer them—and there's your document.

Usually you take out the questions. After a house has been built, you don't see the underlying framework.

Sometimes, however, an architect will achieve an interesting effect by allowing the framework to show. You can do something comparable by leaving the structural questions in the final document.

The finished product will have questions leading into each main section:

Why should we consider a change in the method of following up inquiries?
Our rate of conversion of inquiries from trade advertising has declined 4% in
  eight months. . . .
What's causing the decline?
Two factors are hurting our conversion rate. It takes too long to get leads into the
  hands of salespeople. And some obviously bad leads are not being
  screened out. . . .
Why do these factors hurt us?
Statistical analysis and anecdotal experience show that, after two weeks, the
  viability of these leads drops off rapidly. . . .

Forcing Questions

Leading questions—questions worded in a way that suggests the answer—are used by lawyers to guide witnesses in the desired direction.

You can use purposefully worded questions to influence the attitudes of your audience. For example, a writer asks,

When will your revision be completed?

This is a straightforward request for information. Suppose it's changed to

Will your revision be completed on schedule?

This version puts on a little more pressure. The writer can heighten the pressure with something like this:

Am I correct in assuming your revision will be completed on schedule?

There are other refinements of pressure, like

How far ahead of schedule will you complete your revision? One week? Two
weeks?

When you use a question, think of it not just as a request for an answer but also as a chance to influence the reader.

Leading the Reader—From Most Important to Least Important

Most important to least important is a familiar method of organization. You start with the announcement of a new product and end with the information that it will be packaged in 6- and 12-ounce bottles, the same as the old product.

This organization is okay if the material at the end really is pretty trivial. However, some material may be trivial to one reader but important to another. And even "trivial" information should be read.

So you may want to modify the most-important-to-least-important organization in this way: Start with the most important material (the "lead" in newspaper terms). Then mix up the material that follows. Don't follow a rigorous order, descending to the least significant. If your opening item is important enough, everything that follows should be of equal interest.

Starting in the Middle

Here's a technique that should be used sparingly—but one that can create an interesting effect: *Start in the middle*.

Let's say you're writing a fairly long report that

describes in detail an ongoing procedure.
evaluates the procedure.
recommends changes.

You could start at the beginning:

This report covers the major steps in our present method of handling delinquencies on oil properties.

You could start at the end:

Our approach to handing delinquencies on oil properties should be revised as follows. . . .

A third way to do it:

Our present system of handling delinquencies on oil properties is not working. Here are the reasons for reaching that conclusion. . . .

Now your description of the procedure is read within the context of your judgment that it needs to be changed. Then you follow with a description of the changes that should be made.

This is a change of pace, not a structure to be used habitually. When it's used right, it can make your document more interesting and coherent.

Reversing the Usual Order

Recurring reports tend to fall into patterns. For example, one company's sales operation is organized into seven regions. Certain reports, organized geographically, always follow this order:

Northeast
Atlantic Coastal
Southeast
Central
Southwest
Mountain
Far West

This organization makes it easy for readers to skip over material relating to all the other regions and get right to their own. In a subtle way, the standard organization also tends to "rank" the regions.

When you want readers to look at all parts of a document, or if you're just interested in shaking up the established method of presentation, revise the tacitly established order of such standard formats. Be arbitrary about it. Run the material in random order each time. This eliminates "ranking" and says, in effect, "Everything in this document is of equal importance."

Leading the Reader—From Simple to Complex

Ever watch people at the beach as they first venture into chilly water? Some tiptoe hesitantly. Others take the approach that it's best to get the shock over with all at once, so they race down the sand and dive in.

When you write a document that presents difficult ideas, you have a choice. Should you hurl your readers into the cold water of the most difficult stuff right away? Or should you lead your readers, step by step, from the relative comfort of the easier material to the shock of the difficult?

In most cases the step-by-step approach, leading from simple to more complex material, is better. The reader is given firm footing at the outset and a chance to gradually get used to the shakier footing of the difficult concepts.

A memo on a radar system might begin:

When radio waves are beamed out from a powerful transmitter, they will bounce off any object in their path. A small fraction of the output will be reflected back to a receiver placed next to the transmitter. . . .

From here the memo goes on to explain to a nontechnical audience the principles of an airborne radar that involves an "antenna" formed by several planes flying in formation.

The explanation works better this way than if the writer had started with the newest ideas:

The outstanding feature of this system is the establishment of an airborne ionization grid that registers minute microwave variations in response to responses stimulated by the echo-ranging beam. . . .

Progress from simple to complex is a good organization when dealing with readers who are not experts. Experts, however, will find it boring, even insulting.

Important and Unimportant Documents

Good writing requires effort. This book aims to make it easier to write well, but let's not kid ourselves. There's some work involved.

When you're called on to write something, you're bound to take into account the importance of the document. If it's insignificant, you don't want to devote unnecessary time and effort to it. That's common sense.

The main criterion of importance, of course, is subject matter. When you're reporting a major development, that's important. When you're delivering a critical decision, that's important.

Some people go by length. The longer it is, the more important it is. Not so. A short note on a hot topic can be as vital as a four-page memo. It deserves thought and skill.

Another measure of importance (to the writer) is the audience. When you're writing about something that strikes you as routine, you might be tempted to just toss it off. But if that piece of writing—whatever its intrinsic weight—is read by people whose judgment of you makes a difference, then it's important. If your document will go into a file that may be reviewed by a number of potentially influential persons, then it should be written well. You want to make your point—and look good at the same time.

Consider your own image and reputation as well as the subject matter in deciding the importance of a piece of writing.

Sharpening the "Routine" Memo

The vast majority of the documents sluicing through company channels can be described as "routine." They are part of the customary procedure.

But you should still be precise in writing them. No document is so "routine" that it deserves to be handled sloppily. Everything you write should be written well and written *appropriately*.

Writing appropriately means writing in a way that suits the situation. Let's say you're responding to a routine request for information from higher up. There is nothing extraordinary about the information you're sending back. So it would be *inappropriate* to use a lot of innovative writing techniques. Write crisply; write concisely. But keep your style within the boundaries of the expected.

Here's an example: A division head has asked a departmental manager for information on the progress of several projects. Such requests come periodically. The division head wants to update his files. Unless one of the projects has departed from the track in some way, this is strictly an informational exchange. The division head expects to skim the memo. He doesn't expect to come upon anything unusual.

So the manager starts the memo with an opening used countless times before:

Information on the projects referenced in your 6/183 is enclosed at your request.

A *very* routine opening. You might call it stodgy. But the manager knows her boss. She knows this customary, somewhat stilted opening is right for the circumstances. An unusual opening would suggest that there is something unusual in the accompanying material. Since this is not the case, it's best just to plod along in the usual way.

If the manager wants to give a little more punch to the opening, she might use something like this:

In your 6/183 you asked for an update on three projects. Here's a progress report.

These openings say, in effect this is a response to your request—no more, no less. No surprises.

However, let's say that the manager has found a way to finish one of the projects considerably ahead of schedule. Her opening should alert the recipient to the fact that there *is* something out of the ordinary to report:

Here is a progress report on the three projects you asked about in your 6/183. You'll note that we're going to be able to bring in #17 well ahead of our deadline.

Let's suppose there is *bad* news to report. The departmental manager might be tempted to try to slide it through disguised as "routine" and surrounded by a lot of deadening verbiage. That's a bad idea.

But should bad news be highlighted up front? It depends on the kind of bad news you're talking about. For instance, let's say the manager has run into a temporary setback on one of the projects. She's sure it can be straightened out, and she would prefer not to make a big deal of it at this point. So she writes a totally routine answer to the request for information. She does not alert the division head up front. When she comes to the point in question, she reports the facts and then puts them into perspective:

Our lead supplier of high-impact struts has had an equipment breakdown that will cut output by 60 percent for the next three months. We have selected two alternate suppliers and will make final arrangements with them next week.

This handling says, "You asked what's going on and I'm telling you what's going on. This is a negative development, but it is being handled. Since nothing ever goes perfectly, you can regard this information as routine. No need for you to worry or get involved.''

If, however, the request for an update arrives at just about the time the manager is absorbing the full implications of a major setback, it would be a big mistake to even include this bad news as part of the "routine" update. The manager should first get off a bulletin laying out the facts about the setback. Then send along the routine memo updating all the projects. Any time you look as if you're trying to conceal bad news, you are in trouble.

So there are all sorts of ways of handling the "routine" document, particularly the opening. The key principle is to keep the opening in tune with the situation. If there's nothing unusual in the document, don't signal anything unusual at the outset. If there is something of more than ordinary interest, open the document appropriately.

Who Needs Routine Memos?

Now we need to say something else about "routine" documents. Are they really necessary?

Look at the communications coming to you from those who work for you. How much of it is generated to do a specific job—pass along necessary information, make requests, offer projections? How much of it is so routine as to be zombielike? If people periodically crank out memos and reports just because it's time to do so, then it's time to think about discontinuing the practice.

When you're required to send along routine documents to your boss, you have, of course, less leeway. But you can still take a critical look at the practice. Say, for example, that the departmental manager, asked for a routine report, knows that little if anything happens with this paperwork. She sends along a routine response, adhering scrupulously to the established format. Then she composes an accompanying memo:

> In line with your continuing efforts to streamline operations and build productivity, here is a suggestion about periodic progress reports:
>   Let's switch to shorter, unscheduled reports that focus only on departures from projected progress. This procedure would spare you from reading a lot of routine material and would spare managers from collecting routine information. . . .

Should This Be Put in Writing?

In May 1990, Ford faced a problem. Dealers were becoming increasingly reluctant to stock up on 1990 models, fearing that when the 1991 models appeared in the fall, the dealers would be stuck with a lot of cars.

To stimulate lagging midyear sales, Ford wanted to reassure dealers that, come fall, they would not be forced to take a bath. So Ford decided to guarantee its dealers against catastrophic loss. The manufacturer hit upon a plan to double incentives on 1990 models after the 1991 models appeared.

Ford put this good news into a letter sent to dealers. Everything was fine until the trade journal *Automotive News* disclosed the pledge. Word began to spread outside the industry confines when *The Wall Street Journal, The New York Times,* and other publications reported the arrangement.

For obvious reasons, Ford was unhappy and apprehensive. Even though the company was offering hefty incentives already, car buyers were not flocking into the showrooms. If prospective buyers were sure of enjoying doubled incentives if they waited a few months, why should they buy now? *The Wall Street Journal* ("Ford Plan May Make Buyers Wait," by Gregory A. Patterson, May 17, 1990, p. B1) quoted a Ford spokesman who admitted to being worried that publicity about the fall incentive program would hurt summer sales: "It depends to a large extent on the degree to which [the plans are] reported."

Ford had detailed a potentially damaging plan in a letter that was sent to dealers all over the country—without fully considering the possibility that the news would become public.

Before sending the letter to dealers, *Ford should have made the assumption that the letter would become widely known.* This is an essential assumption to make about *any* broadly distributed communication—especially one that goes outside the organization.

The notion that somehow the lid can be kept on written messages is pervasive. Even when the message goes to a lot of addressees whose reactions cannot be controlled, the originator still clings to the comforting idea that the contents won't get out because it would be inconvenient. Ford seems to have cherished this mistaken assumption even when this potentially hot information was being sent to dealers who were not happy and who would not bend over backwards to protect the manufacturer.

You have some controversial or potentially dangerous material to transmit. Ask yourself some hard questions:

How many people is this addressed to?
Who else will see it?
What happens if the message is seen by
   a reporter?
   a competitor?
   a regulator?
   a "business watchdog"?

the person or persons most negatively affected?

the staff of your company?

those whom you would *least* like to see it?

Could someone "break security" to hurt you? Or the company?

Are you certain enough that the message will not be seen by the wrong eyes?

Now, apply a "worst case" approach. What's the worst thing that can happen if this information reaches unwelcome eyes? Personal embarrassment? Damage to your image? Damage to the company? A possible lawsuit? Unpleasant publicity? Customer backlash? All of the above?

When you send a sensitive message to a fairly broad audience or to people whom you can't rely on to keep it confidential, then you're taking a risk. It becomes an exercise in risk assessment. Maybe the necessity to get the message out overrides the risk. If so, be aware that the document may get into the wrong hands and plan accordingly. If Ford had assumed that the incentive plan would become public knowledge, it might still have sent out the letter. But Ford should not have been surprised that the letter became public.

Or maybe there's another way to pass the most sensitive stuff along; maybe it doesn't have to be written out in detail. The Ford letter probably would have been okay if it had been more general, assuring dealers that the company had plans to prevent the buildup of a glut of 1990 cars. The most sensitive details might have been passed along by word of mouth from Ford representatives to the dealers. True, this process would take longer and be more cumbersome, but it would avoid the damaging words on paper. And it's also true that one or more dealers might have told trade journalists that Ford might sweeten the incentive pot in the fall. But hearsay is different from the "smoking gun" of a document that spells it all out. Ford could have handled rumors of beefed-up incentives; there are always rumors. It was the specificity of the letter that did the damage.

Before sending "hot" material by a written message, look into all possibilities of passing it along by word of mouth. The best solution may be a combination: a written message that gives the broad outlines and invites the recipient to ask about details and applications.

When you put it in writing, you give up a large measure of control over what you've said. If there's a real chance that your words can come back to haunt you, think twice—maybe three times.

CHAPTER 3

Dress Your Words for Success: Style and Clarity

The style is the person, according to the Comte de Buffon, the great French naturalist. You have a style in looks, dress, speech. You have a writing style as well. It may be a clumsy style, a pedestrian style, a blah style—whatever. If you're a quick resourceful, forceful person, and your written messages don't represent you as quick, resourceful, and forceful, then you are undermining yourself with everything you write.

And besides, your writing isn't getting the job done.

This chapter is a *catalog of stylistic strategies.* Use it to find—and adapt—techniques that give your written words distinction and impact.

Should Business Documents Be Fun?

Some people are entertaining to listen to, even when they're talking about very serious things. Irreverent jokes . . . caustic asides . . . earthy interjections—you listen with heightened interest because you never know what you're going to hear next.

Some people, on the other hand, are dull speakers, even when they're talking about things of great inherent interest. Your boss is talking about an impending change that will affect you. He speaks clearly, covers the details in logical order, presents reasonable arguments. But everything is predictable, juiceless, monotonic. You listen because it's important. But you have to force yourself.

Business writing tends to make everybody seem dull. People who sparkle when speaking dim their luster when writing. When you read their letters, reports, and memos you see nothing of the liveliness of the author.

There are reasons for this dullness, of course. It's one thing to be irreverent, surprising, provocative, and funny when you're talking with someone. You see the other person's reaction, sense whether your words are being received the way you intend them. When you write you shoot arrows off into the blue. Another reason is the cautious approach adopted by business writers. They tend to write defensively. Any departure from the formula is risky. They understand that an essential element is the successful management of risks, big and small. They're willing to take chances in all sorts of areas because they're confident of their ability. But not in writing.

We look out over a monotonous gray landscape of document writing. People read the messages; they have to. But it's a chore, and sometimes it's hard work. It's certainly not much fun.

So writers who inject even a tiny dose of fun into their documents can make a vivid impression. When everything is gray, a touch of bright color stands out sharply. Erasmus said, "In the country of the blind the one-eyed man is king."

Let's look at some ways in which you can add those interesting touches of color that will increase attention and convey personality.

Some Buzzwords Don't Travel Well

When buzzwords are on everyone's lips—and when everyone understands what they mean—it's okay to use them. But buzzwords (or buzzterms) lack precision. They soar into prominence like skyrockets and quickly dissolve into a blur. Terms like "management by objectives" become so diffuse that they are virtually useless—or even misleading. Peter Drucker, who pioneered the concept of management by objectives, deplores the fact that the words are often taken to mean imposing bottom-line requirements on managers without being concerned about how they accomplish those objectives.

Some terms become local buzzwords. They mean something specific inside the organization. Here's part of a letter to a customer:

> You'll be happy to hear that your agreement to this new procedure will mean an upgrade for you.

Within the writer's company, "upgrade" has a special meaning. It covers a package of benefits conferred on certain favored customers: additional discounts, guaranteed delivery, etc. There has been a lot of discussion of the upgrade concept. Customers have been informed of the details of the policy. So the author of this letter thinks the addressee knows all about it.

But the addressee doesn't know all about it. "Upgrade" could mean anything, including mere hype. So the promise has no impact.

Before using a buzzword, ask yourself if there is any possibility that the audience—or any part of the audience—may not be familiar with it.

"Household Words" That Not Everyone Knows

You can certainly make messages shorter by simply making a brief reference to something that is thoroughly familiar to all parties. When there's no need to spell something out at length, don't do it.

But be careful. Be sure that everybody is really familiar with the material you are referring to in shorthand. For example:

Rollout will proceed according to the enclosed timetable. As agreed, we will monitor and compare observations along the lines of the Nashville Plan.

The "Nashville Plan" is a procedure developed at a conference in Nashville that was attended by the sender and the main addressee. As far as the main addressee is concerned, the reference is perfectly clear. But there are others involved in implementation of the plan—and they did *not* attend the Nashville conference. They may have heard about it—but they don't know all the details. Therefore the message is incomplete.

When there's any possibility that your cryptic reference may not be clear, fill out the details. Think, not just about the principal addressees, but about others who may read what you've written.

"Familiar" Sayings That Are Unfamiliar

A manager is commenting on the fact that a report is short on substance. He starts his memo by saying:

My first reaction to this document is to ask, "Where's the beef?"

Familiar expressions, when used properly, can be quite effective. They give a down-to-earth, conversational tone to your writing. They're a kind of shorthand; by using slang you can get a point across in fewer words than would be required by more formal language.

But you must be absolutely sure the reader understands the slang. It has to be so current that it's on everybody's lips or so universal that there can be no question of misunderstanding.

In this case, the writer used "Where's the beef?" to mean "Where's the substance?" The line comes from a hamburger-chain commercial of the 1980s that was borrowed by Walter Mondale to attack Gary Hart in the presidential primary campaign of 1984.

Most people still understand the term in that sense. But by now it's old enough so that some readers will not get it. In this case the reader took "beef" to mean "complaint." He spent a good deal of time trying to understand why the boss was asking, "What are you complaining about?"

Subject slang expressions to a "worst-case" test. If it's possible that they can be misunderstood, don't use them.

Approximately . . . Nearly . . . About—Coming Close

There are interesting shades of meaning among words meaning similarity but not identity. Contrast these usages:

I expect that we'll gross around $4M.
Costs will be approximately $60,000.
Projections lead us to expect scores on the order of 65–70 percent.

"Around" is casual. The writer seems to be saying, "This is what I figure it will be without taking too much trouble to figure it out." When "approximately" is used, the connotation is somewhat more precise. The word implies a process of analysis applied to reaching the stated figure.

"On the order of" is a faintly pedantic usage that means "around" or "about" but suggests that the estimate should be given considerable weight because of the gravity and authority of the writer. Purists denounce usages like "on the order of." But let's not be too hasty. Sometimes people are impressed by such language, and such reactions can come in handy.

Sports Terms: When—and When Not—to Use Them

The parallels between sports and business are obvious and well-worn. Some people use athletic terms weirdly: "You can't ice-skate on a basketball court," declares an executive. His meaning is clear to him but obscure to the audience.

Terms like "good field position" and "full-court press" are pretty familiar, even to those who are not avid followers of football or basketball. Stay away from terms that require the audience to be familiar with the sport. The marketing manager who urges a subordinate to "serve an ace" assumes everyone knows that tennis term, but a subordinate might not have a clue.

Sports terms work—when they're familiar—because they're visually descriptive. Sometimes they can be felt in the gut. A manager might say, "Mr. Werber looked as if the meeting had taken quite a toll on him." However, he's likely to achieve more impact if he writes, "After the meeting, Mr. Werber looked as if he'd gone fifteen rounds with Mike Tyson."

This also applies to military terms. "Establish a beachhead," "take the high ground," and "outflank" are familiar to almost everyone. But a manager who writes "We'll take them under enfilading fire" misses the target.

When a sports or military term—or an analogy—pops readily into your head and seems perfectly relevant, use it. Never reach for it.

Using Analogies to Make Your Point

Analogies—or parables or fables—are brief stories that draw a moral or make a point. The parable of the Good Samaritan, the legend of the tortoise and the hair, the fable of the fox and the grapes—these stories express ideas that we can apply to other problems and other endeavors.

Don't reach too far for analogies, but when an analogy fits perfectly into your message, use it. Analogies in business writing should be short. They should be instantly recognizable to the reader. They should be unmistakably relevant to the matter at hand. For instance, a manager wants to impress the staff with the importance of being alert to accidental possibilities:

> Let's keep awake to the opportunities for improvement. Sometimes the unexpected tells us valuable things. When Charles Goodyear dropped a mixture of India rubber and sulfur on a hot stove, he discovered the process of vulcanization. Goodyear made that discovery because his mind was alert to the possibilities.

Comics Kids and Other Popular Culture Figures

An executive writes:

> In June 1988 we were given the mission of preparing the market for introduction of a new low-end line. The preparation went well, but design and production ran into problems, and the project was aborted. In the fall of 1990 we were led to believe that our franchising agreement would be revised to provide dealers with more favorable terms on exclusives. That didn't happen. Now there is the possibility that we may reduce prices, and we're asked to pass that word along. I'm tired of having Lucy pull the football away just as I go to kick it.

The executive wants to say something pretty hard-nosed in a non-hard-nosed way. The reference to Charles Schulz's "Peanuts" characters comes in handy. Practically everyone knows that the eternal children of "Peanuts" play out the same mythic patterns over and over again, and that one of the most vivid is Charlie Brown's futile somersault as he falls victim once again to Lucy's trick.

Popular culture figures, including comic characters and TV figures like J. R. of "Dallas," have become part of our contemporary folklore. You can use them to good effect in making points.

Quantify Wherever Possible

Precision beats generality every time. "The *Fortune* 500" is better than "a lot of big companies." "Some Techniques for Achieving Success" sounds all right; "Sixteen Ways to Become President within Five Years" packs more punch.

Whenever you can quantify a proposition, you give it texture and solidity. There are ways to quantify statements even when you don't have exact figures. Instead of "A substantial number of prospects see our outdoor advertising," say:

More than 63 percent of our potential buyers see our billboards and posters.

Sometimes you can find the basis for quantification in the preparation that went into a prediction or a proposal:

This projection is supported by 1,263 hours of staff work.

There's a tendency to round off numbers: approximately 1,000 instead of 994, ten principles rather than nine or eleven. Don't round off. When you're making lists, look for unrounded numbers:

Seven Steps for Handling Complaints
Twelve Danger Signs in Loan Applications

Contrasting Construction

You want to contrast two sets of items—past with present, false with true, bad with good. You can achieve impact by dividing the document (or the relevant section of it) into parallel columns of brief blocks of copy:

The Old Way	The New Way
Call reports were as much as a week late.	Call reports will be sent daily.
Mail leads piled up at the home office until they were sent in bulk to the field.	Mail leads will be processed as they come, screened, and sent by the end of the next day.
Customer Service operated independently of Field Sales.	Customer Service activities will be coordinated with Field Sales.

Signal Negative Comments in Advance

You're writing a commentary on a report by a subordinate. Your observations are 95 percent favorable. However, there is one error that has to be corrected. Your memo proceeds for a couple of pages. Only then does it get to the difficulty:

> Here I have to point out the one shortcoming of this otherwise good plan. Your figures are based on the loan experience in New York and New Jersey. These figures should not be extrapolated. . . .

The trouble here is that the recipient, lulled into a pleasant stupor by the foregoing favorable comments, skims over the negative comment.

Signal what you're doing at the beginning:

> Here are my comments on your report. With one exception, they contain amplification of your points, which are excellent. The one exception comes at Step 8, where I question your figures.
>
> Overall, this is a very sound approach.
>
> Step 1—Your premise is reasonable . . .

"This" Is Not Good Enough

> Our Product Improvement Program is an effective method for integrating the quality development, improvement, and maintenance efforts of the various functional groups within the company's organization. This enables design, production, and test at the most cost-effective levels and allows for full customer satisfaction. This concept recognizes that performance of the quality function is inherent in all phases of the company's operation. This program is common to all employees from the executive level on down.

The foregoing excerpt from a corporate document demonstrates the result of overreliance on "this" as a handy substitute for the subject. Result? Vagueness and dullness.

The passage is vague because "this" changes its meaning slightly with each repetition. The passage is dull because a series of sentences starting with "this" put the reader to sleep. Without revising the paragraph in any other way, let's try to clear up the "this" problem:

> Our Product Improvement Program is an effective method for integrating the quality development, improvement, and maintenance efforts of the various functional groups within the company's organization. The program enables design, production, and test at the most cost-effective levels and allows for full customer satisfaction. The underlying concept of the Product Improvement Program recognizes that performance of the quality function is inherent in all

phases of the company's operation. The program involves all employees from the executive level on down.

Quoting the Right Authority

Choosing the right quotation helps in two ways. An apt quote from a credible authority adds to the force of an argument. And, since quotation is a form of tribute, those who are quoted tend to look favorably on the person doing the quoting.

Keep a file of potentially useful statements and comments by senior members of management and influential people in the organization. The file may consist of correspondence, excerpts from speeches, articles, press releases, parts of the proceedings of meetings. At the apt moment, use the right quote.

For example, a division head is pushing hard to get some new equipment. Here's how he strengthens his case:

> These machines will pay for themselves within a relatively short period, considering the benefits they give us. In addition to the reduction of downtime and the increased speed, we will be equipping ourselves for the twenty-first century. As Roger Umphlett commented recently, "Reliable process control is the wave of the future. This company will be second to none in taking advantage of technological advances in our field."

Roger Umphlett is the chairman and CEO. He made this fairly general comment in a speech, and the writer has applied it to this argument. At the very least, the writer is allying himself with the chairman in a brave march into the future. And the quotation may well carry considerable weight with the writer's immediate boss (who may not know the exact source of the citation).

When You Quote from a Book, Identify It

In referring to authority, identify the source—not only the person, but also, when relevant, the book or article:

> Peter Drucker says, "We will have to learn to lead people rather than to contain them" (Management: Tasks, Responsibilities, Practices, Harper & Row, 1974).

This citation gives readers a chance to read the book if interested. You don't have to give the page of the quote unless you distinctly want the other person to read that passage. If you give a page number, note the edition (hardcover, etc.).

Credit All Your Sources

We are contemptuous of people who deliberately take credit for the accomplishments of others. But some people appropriate the work of others without realizing what they're doing.

When you write a document that depends to some degree on the contributions of colleagues or subordinates, give credit where credit is due. Sometimes we forget the source of input. Review what you're writing to make sure you're not taking credit for something that should be credited to someone else. Be generous with credit. Whenever it's a borderline question whether to mention somebody's name, mention it. You please the other person, you get credit for fairness—and you do the right thing.

Work in references to the contributions of others by quotation:

As Art Fletcher observes, "Fuel capacity will become a decisive factor in the sale."

Or just give credit by name:

Maud Fitzpatrick of the Kansas City office discovered that . . .

Never Say "Never" (or "Always")

When you're tempted to make a blanket statement, allowing for no exceptions, think about qualifying it. Absolute certainty is almost always suspect:

We will never be undersold.
Our account people always respond the same day.
Cover every retail outlet in the region.

Absolute statements are almost always invalid because, somewhere, sometime there is an exception. However, even when absolutes are (in the writer's opinion) valid, they should be avoided if the reader is going to question them. For example:

We sell to all members of the <u>Fortune</u> 500.

That statement may be literally true—at least at the moment it's written. But it stops the reader, who wonders if there isn't at least one exception. Why raise doubts in the reader's mind, even when the statement is true? Qualify it:

We sell to virtually all members of the <u>Fortune</u> 500.

Absolute certainty, even when justified, can damage credibility.

If You Say It, You Don't Have to Say You Believe It

Everything you write should be credible. So why assert your own confidence in certain statements?

> I firmly believe that our selection procedure meets organizational needs.
> It is my firm believe that the equipment will stand up under desert conditions.
> In my opinion there is likely to be a considerable backlash in reaction to these ads.

In the first example, the first four words weaken the statement. (The writer doth protest too much.) The second example is a supposition, so it may be all right to label it as such. But use fewer words. "I think" or "I believe" will do the job. Since the third statement contains a qualifier ("is likely to be"), the "In my opinion" opening is unnecessary.

There are times when this sort of added-on assurance serves a purpose—for example, when the writer is refuting other assertions:

> The suit alleges that we lag behind local standards in our hiring practices. <u>As a matter of fact</u>, we exceed those standards.

> These days we hear more and more about the permanent decline of commercial real estate in this area. I firmly believe we are due for an upturn . . .

As a General Rule This Term Is Redundant

Rules apply generally throughout the areas of their relevance. Otherwise they wouldn't be rules. So "as a general rule" is redundant. Use one word or the other:

> As a rule we meet the first Thursday of each month.
> Generally we meet the first Thursday . . .

Watch for other common redundancies:

ultimate outcome
advance planning
local resident
root cause
separate compartments
enthusiastic fans
temporary postponement

Mini-Definitions—Sometimes They Help, Sometimes They Don't

The mini-definition is an explanatory term stuck unobtrusively in a sentence:

Siemens is a German company with a multinational reach.

The mini-definition "is a German Company" has a function here. The writer is not sure the reader knows where Siemens is based. To spell it out as a separate sentence ("Siemens is a German company") might insult a reader who already knows it ("What does he think I am, a dummy?"). To leave it out might lead to an erroneous conclusion. So the writer slips in the useful mini-definition as part of a sentence that makes another point.

Sometimes mini-definitions are obvious or self-evident:

Chicago is a city in which . . .
He is a man who . . .

Eliminate mini-definitions that spell out the obvious.

"To Tell the Truth"—Better Leave It Out

Certain expressions, fairly common in speech, appear occasionally in business writing, particularly when the document is being dictated. For example, halfway through a memo reporting on a visit to a division, the writer says:

To tell the truth, I had the feeling that they are still apprehensive about the goals for the coming year.

"To tell the truth" does nothing—except maybe to imply that the foregoing material is a lie. Here's another one:

Up to this point I have covered the personnel and equipment requirements of the proposed task force. Let's face facts: some of these requirements will be extremely hard to meet.

"Let's face facts" can be said with a disarming smile and gesture. When the words are written, they go further than the writer intended in implying that the foregoing material is, to some extent, fiction.

Such terms can, and should, be eliminated from business documents.

Run Simple Sentences Together

Simple sentences get the job done, as in the following:

We are moving the Customer Relations staff to the WhiteWay location. The move will be completed by August 18. Customer Relations will occupy the fifth floor. This space has been vacant since Audit III was transferred to the East Coast. We are installing computers, fax, and telex.

This jerky prose is the equivalent of stick figures in drawing. The facts are clear, but it's hard to read. The message is important, but the simplistic way in which it's presented diminishes the importance.

Sometimes it's useful to put things down in a series of simple sentences in order to make sure you're covering everything in the right sequence. Read over what you've written. Then, if it looks too rudimentary, combine the material into more complex sentences that show the relationships:

We are moving the Customer Relations staff to the fifth floor at the WhiteWay location, vacant since Audit III was transferred to the East Coast. Computers, fax, and telex are being installed in the space, which Customer Relations will occupy by August 18.

If It's "Self-explanatory," You don't Have to Say So

Supervisors within the financial division of a company receive a message from the vice-president for finance:

In order to bring uniformity to the reporting of computer malfunctions, we have prepared the attached outline.

The outline should be self-explanatory and should be followed in reporting computer problems . . .

The words "should be self-explanatory" are not helpful. In fact they may be harmful. What is self-explanatory to the person who originates the material may not be self-explanatory to the person who has to understand it. When the term is used like this it acts as a deterrent to questions. A reader who doesn't understand the message may be reluctant to ask questions, because asking questions about the "self-explanatory" makes you look dumb.

Try to make everything self-explanatory. But don't label anything this way. Instead, invite legitimate questions:

We have tried to make this outline as easy to use as possible. Please look it over carefully. If you have any questions, ask them . . .

No Fake Sentiment

"I know you welcome frank criticism," begins the memo, which proceeds to point out some areas in which the recipient is not performing up to standard.

Has anyone in the history of the world actually *welcomed* criticism, frank or otherwise? Such glib formulations just irritate the person being criticized. In the same way, the person on the other end is not likely to enjoy being told, "You will want to learn the full extent of the failure right away."

When you have bad news to deliver, deliver it dispassionately and clearly. You may want to mitigate its force by putting it in perspective, balancing it with praise, and so on. That's up to you. But avoid the insincerity of meaningless attributions of delight at bad news.

Inventing a Word That's Already Invented

People sometimes create new words because they sound logical. One problem with such inventiveness is that the resulting word may sound peculiar. Yet another, and more serious problem, may be that the word is already "taken"—given another meaning.

Case in point: In 1990 the major television networks disclosed that they wanted to install new systems for counting the number of viewers watching their shows. The traditional measurements—the Nielson ratings—showed that network viewing was declining sharply, resulting in the loss of millions of dollars. The networks were considering alternate methods that would, no doubt, be less harsh than the Nielsons in imposing the necessity to run free commercials to reach the guarantees.

Advertising agencies were furious, proclaiming that the networks wanted to change the rules because they were losing the game. In the midst of this controversy, NBC called the new plan "*actionable* and equitable."

"*Actionable!*" The NBC spokesperson, in using this word to defend the change, meant that the idea was doable or workable. Maybe "actionable" seemed like a better word, meaning lending itself to effective action.

But the word "actionable" has a specific meaning: "subject or liable to a lawsuit."

Certainly NBC did not mean to suggest that it could be sued for putting in the new plan. But that's the way it came out. When you're tempted to use an invented word, *look it up.*

Beware the Unassigned Task

After making some comments on a proposed course of action, a manager writes:

This looks good to me, but let's not proceed until Henry Grunwald has a chance to look at it.

Nothing happens. Some time later, the author of these words asks the addressee if the plan has been implemented. The would-be implementer has been waiting for the other guy to check it out with Grunwald. And vice versa.

Whenever you suggest action—particularly new action—spell out who's going to do it and, if necessary, how it should be done. A clear instruction is especially important when the suggested action is difficult. It happens that, in this example, Grunwald was hard to reach. The author hoped the addressee would do it, without being willing to instruct the addressee to do it.

Unassigned tasks are orphans. Never assume the other guy is going to do something that is not spelled out.

Apples and Oranges

When you make a comparison, the two things being compared must be logically comparable:

The research department at Southeast is superior to any other region in the company.

This sentence compares one part, research, to entire regions. It should read:

The research department at Southeast is superior to the research department of any other region in the company.

Incomplete comparisons may be confusing as well as sloppy:

We use temporaries more than Central Assembly.

This could mean:

We use temporaries more than Central Assembly uses temporaries.

Or it could mean:

We use temporaries more than we use Central Assembly.

Spell it out.

Tabularize for Easy Reading

Look for opportunities to ''bullet'' suitable material. Here's a paragraph that needs the shot in the arm that bulleting provides:

> This micro gives every workstation the capacity to work with the system as if each had a separate computer, while sharing resources like disk storage, data communication, and printers. Each user has a dedicated processor and memory. The system works with almost all makes of printer. IBM compatibility is another distinct advantage. We have access to an extensive range of software . . .

When you're running through a number of similar points that support an overarching point, bullet the points and indent them. This format sends a signal to the reader that the individual points are components in a larger concept. It also makes the material easier to read:

> This micro gives us a number of advantages that permit users to work with the system as if each had an individual computer, while sharing basic resources. Advantages include
>
> - dedicated processor and memory for each user.
> - the ability to work with almost all makes of printer.
> - IBM compatibility.
> - access to an extensive range of software.

Make Headings Specific

Generic headings like ''Summary'' and ''Background'' are uninformative. They're also dull. They say, ''This is a routine document, like a hundred others you've read recently.''

Give your headings more variety and greater specificity:

> Factors Bearing on the Problem
> Market Trends
> How We Got to This Point
> Pivotal Points
> Interesting Angles
> Basis for the Conclusion
> Where We Are, Where We're Going
> What We Need to Do

Make your heads conversational, specific, and inviting. Such headings add warmth and encourage the reader to go on.

What Did They Say?

When we read novels, most of us like to turn the page and discover quotation marks. We enjoy "listening" to the characters speaking, rather than making our way through paragraphs of solid prose that tell us what they said.

Occasional use of direct quotes can build readership in your correspondence. Instead of this:

> Diamond instructed the sales force to focus more attention on convenience stores in shore localities during the summer months.

You might write this:

> "Go after the convenience stores in the beach towns," Diamond told the sales force.

Make sure the quote is accurate, of course.

Quotes make a document more readable. And they can have a greater impact on the reader than paraphrases, especially when the reader knows the person being quoted. The quoted words evoke the look and tone of the speaker.

Highlighting the "Fine Print"

A dealer is considering a franchise arrangement with a manufacturer. He is plowing through a long document spelling out the terms of the exclusive arrangement. Buried deep in the document he comes upon a section beginning:

> Pursuant to Section IX, Paragraph 4 of the Understanding, the Dealer undertakes to accept minimum shipment quotas on new or revised product lines issued by the Manufacturer, such undertakings to include . . .

"Aha! Here's the 'fine print'!" The dealer reacts to this section with far more suspicion than is warranted, because it seems to him to have been slipped in with the hope that he won't notice.

When you are including "downside" material in a document (especially a long document) that is essentially positive in tone, *highlight it*. Dispel the notion that you are trying to get away with something. Move the section toward the front. Introduce it with some clarifying words, for example:

> This section spells out performance requirements for both parties and possible penalties for nonperformance. While this is a necessary part of any such agreement, we can put it in perspective by . . .

Your readers will spot the "fine print" stuff anyway. Win points by calling attention to it.

Incongruous Mixtures

After visiting a branch office, a manager writes to the branch head:

Dear Jerry,

I enjoyed our get-together last week. You and your gang seem well embarked on a course that will turn things around fast. You can count on us to give you the help you're going to need.

A package of materials relating to revised plans for next fiscal year has been sent to your office. Please inform this office upon receipt of the materials.

The writer wants to hit a warm, informal note. The first paragraph does this, but the second paragraph is stiff and formal.

The second paragraph is a "standard" paragraph, appended to all kinds of messages about transmissions of material. Paragraphs like this can be generated by the touch of a word-processor key. This method saves time, but it can make for an incongruous mix.

When you're writing in a certain tone, keep the tone consistent. In this case, instead of using the standard paragraph, the author might have said:

Tying in with the plans we talked about, I'm sending you some material that you may find helpful. Let me know when you get it.

It's a good idea to review the "standard" paragraphs that are used over and over again. Do they fit all circumstances? While they cover the facts, are they too formal for some messages?

When you're writing informally, make sure that you are informal all the way through. One *pro forma* lapse spoils the effect.

The Cloak of "Facility"

Once, in the pre-TV days, there was a character on radio called the Shadow, who had the power to "cloud men's minds."

Certain words have a mind-clouding quality. They refer to real things, but they don't help us to think about those real things.

The word "facility" is an example. "Transportation facilities" might mean trucks and loading docks; "storage facilities" might mean closets or warehouses; "conference facilities" are hotels with meeting rooms.

"Facility" is useful because it covers a lot of ground without requiring a lot of words. When you're making a passing reference to something, the term gets the job done:

Along with our extensive service facilities, we have a well-trained and responsive customer relations staff . . .

When you really want to focus on the topic, specify what "facility" means:

Our service facilities, which include twenty repair trucks, drivers who are qualified technicians, and a computerized parts warehouse . . .

Give the specifics the first time, then use "facility" throughout the rest of the document.

"Money" Can Be a Four-Letter Word

When the subject of money comes up—particularly when it's a question of paying more money—people flee to euphemisms. A congressman talks about "revenue enhancement." A high school gym teacher talks about "towel upkeep increasement factor."

So, when you write bluntly about money, your words have great impact because they contrast with the mush that is often written about this topic. For example, here's a passage from a corporate memorandum:

The proposed course of action constitutes upward modification of costs that will exert a negative effect on earning capacity in the immediate future.

Try this:

The proposed action will cost too much. We can't afford it.

Superfluous Explanations

"Who" and "which" are often used in identifying people or things:

Johnson, who is the most experienced brand manager in the division . . .
Radio spots, which were used to supplement the network TV advertising . . .

The sentence moves along more briskly when you eliminate these words:

Johnson, the most experienced brand manager . . .
Radio spots, used to supplement . . .

"Who is" and "which were" are understood. You can dispense with them.

The "Ize" Have It

Some purists cringe when a noun is turned into a verb by adding "ize." "Finalize" is the usage that is criticized most.

This is excessive pickiness. "Ize" is useful. There is no good one-word alternative to "finalize" in many of its uses. Computerize . . . legitimize . . . legalize—these words work.

In fact, it may be possible to invent verbs for use within the organization by employing the three letters. For example, a company sometimes turns difficult questions of patent and copyright infringement over to a fellow named Herbert Johnson. A manager writes "Let's Johnsonize this." It's a handy, informal way of making a point that is understood by everyone within the organization.

Save Your Best Punch for the End (of the Sentence)

You build a powerful sentence by placing the most important words at the end. Take this sentence:

This department has met the budget for volume and net profit, although it has fallen short in average calls per week.

Put the payoff words at the end:

Although this department has fallen short in average calls per week, it has met the budget for volume and net profit.

Firecrackers are most impressive when the biggest bang comes last.

Change of Pace—Formal to Informal

The change of pace is one of the most effective ploys of baseball pitchers. The pitcher throws a couple of fastballs—then comes in with a slow change-up.

You can use a version of the change of pace to good effect in writing, as in this excerpt from a marketing executive's memo:

A review of the operating expenses currently charged to this department reveals that these expenses include subexpense classifications as follows: salesmen's salaries and commissions, travel and entertainment, payroll costs, dealer's commissions, manager's salaries and commissions, clerical salaries, communications charges, rent, interest, research salaries and expenses, storage, provision for doubtful accounts, general administrative.
This is a ripoff! We're carrying costs that should not be charged to us. . . .

After a succession of formal terms, the writer throws in the slangy zinger.

When your document contains a lot of necessary but routine stuff, look for the chance to liven things up with a change of pace—a short, punchy sentence that snaps the reader awake.

CHAPTER 4

Wordplay: Special
Strategies and Subtleties

Most people speak more colorfully and adventurously than they write. Our talking vocabularies are larger than our writing vocabularies. This section examines some special areas of wordplay—how to choose the right words, how to deploy those words, what words to leave out.

Stick to the Language You Know

Line managers have always had problems communicating with scientists, specialists, and technicians. The experts speak a special language. It's a language they understand. It expresses ideas in a useful shorthand.

Sometimes experts like to baffle the uninitiated by using the special language. When the line manager is confronted with complex jargon, there's a difficult choice: act as if you understand it, look it up, or ask that it be restated in understandable English. All too often, managers act as if they are at home with the arcane words of the experts, nodding in agreement while they are actually totally at sea.

Experts love this. They know unerringly when a lay person is pretending to be an insider.

Another temptation is to show the experts that you can *speak* their language. It's ludicrous to see a nonlinguist using fractured French to order a meal in a French restaurant. It's equally ludicrous to see a line manager using words like the following to a research scientist:

Since the nitrogenous bases are inconsistent with each other in size, the adenine unit can approximate a thynine or a cytosine, but not a guanine . . .

If this stuff is accurate the scientist thinks scornfully that the manager copied the words out of a book. If it's inaccurate, the manager looks even more foolish.

Don't fake it. The manager should admit ignorance and get to the point:

As best I can understand it, some units are compatible and some are not. Therefore . . .

In writing to people who use a specialized language, stick to your *own* specialized language: *clear, expressive English*. Write without pretense or apology. And require that others write the same way.

Using Impressive Jargon

Most writing teachers struggle to squeeze the jargon out of their students' work. In business, however, there are times when jargon helps you to achieve the effect you want.

A young media director has been assigned by her agency to work with a client whose senior executives may be uncomfortable about her lack of experience. Ordinarily the media director would make her first presentation in plain English. Instead, she includes passages like this:

"We look for our TV flight to give us net reach of 94 with more than four mil Gross Impressions. This gives us 238 GRPs, assuring us that we're reaching enough of our target market with sufficient frequency. In January HUT level peaks, since there are more Households Using Television when the weather is cold . . ."

Command of jargon denotes authority. The media director is establishing her credibility. And it works. The reaction is, "She knows what she's talking about."

Note that the media director provides a kind of simultaneous translation: ". . . assuring us that we're reaching enough of our target market . . . more Households Using Television when the weather is cold . . ."

Where it's useful, *show that you know the jargon. Then put it into words anybody can understand.*

Giving a Running Translation of Jargon

Sometimes you have to communicate with two audiences at the same time—one of which is well-versed in the subject, one of which is not. If you write at the level of the sophisticates, you bewilder the novices. If you gear your writing down to the novices, the sophisticates get bored.

This is an excerpt from a memo on office cost-cutting measures:

Compose and store before uploading—Some members of the department are
still typing out and modifying documents *after* they've made the E-mail
connection. This practice runs up the charge needlessly. Please compose your
document, make all changes, and then upload it from storage.

This message is perfectly clear to those at the workstations. But the memo
is also going to the executive vice-president, who has requested some cost-
reduction moves but who is not familiar with all aspects of using a desktop
terminal. To him this is gibberish.

The solution is to weave in a "running translation."

Keep E-mail charges down—Some members of the department are still making
the E-mail connection (which starts the meter running) and then composing and
revising the material to be sent via E-mail. The better way is to compose the
document and make all the changes *before* connecting to E-mail. When you
have your finished document on a disk, connect and transmit from the disk. This
takes far less time.

Limpwords Are Wimpwords

Limpwords. They trudge across the page, burdening the eyes and brain of
the reader. Some of the prime culprits:

ahead of schedule (early)
a large proportion of (many)
a percentage of (some)
during the time that (while)
at this point in time (now)
in advance of (before)
take action (act)
make use of (use)

These expressions are not redundant or ungrammatical, but they should
be avoided because they dull the responses of the person on the receiving end.
Say the suspect terms aloud:

"We will make an approach to Polaris Products at an early date."

When you hear yourself speak this sentence you're likely to realize that it
can move faster:

"We will approach Polaris Products soon."

As we discuss elsewhere, there are times when weightier language is an effective tactic. Usually, though, *you'll write more vigorously without the limpwords.*

In Defense of Clichés

Platitudes are the pariahs of writing instruction. Trite expressions are denounced, condemned, and sentenced to banishment. However, there are times when it's better to use a cliché than to try to avoid its use.

For example:

There has been little competitive reaction so far, but we think this lack of reaction is a misleading prelude to a period of very heavy activity.

At first the author was going to write:

There has been little competitive reaction so far, but we think this is the calm before the storm.

The latter sentence—in spite of the cliché—does the job better. It takes advantage of familiarity to make its point more clearly and in fewer words.

It's good to avoid clichés, but it's bad to bend over backwards to avoid them. Familiar terms have a useful function. After all, truisms get that way because they are true.

Keep your *thinking* fresh, always. *When you decide that a cliché will work best, use it.*

Slang as Shorthand

The manager has concluded that a proposed new product will not win favor in the marketplace, and that the results will be bad. She might express it this way:

The Magnotherm is being introduced into a highly competitive market. We will be rolling it out with a great deal of promotional fanfare. However, I'm afraid that Magnotherm sales will fall considerably short of projections, resulting not only in financial loss but also in loss of prestige for the company.

Instead, she puts it this way:

I'm afraid the Magnotherm is an Edsel.

When you're sure all your readers will understand it, you can use an informal or slangy term to get an idea across more concisely and vividly than if you spelled it out in more "correct" language.

Tips from Two Old Greeks

How can you use the Socratic method in writing a business document?

Socrates conversed with his students in questions and answers that led the student along toward a conclusion. When you want to lead the reader to a specific conclusion, you might use questions and answers in the same way.

How exactly did Socrates do it?

Plato, Socrates' student, recorded his teacher's methods in Dialogues like the following (quoted from *Plato,* Harvard University Press, Vol. 1, p. 245, translated by Harold North Fowler, 1971):

> When anything becomes greater it must inevitably have been smaller?
>
> Yes.
>
> And the weaker is generated from the stronger, and the slower from the quicker?
>
> That is true.
>
> And the worse from the better and the more just from the more unjust?
>
> Of course.
>
> Then have we established that all things are generated in this way, opposites from opposites?
>
> Certainly . . .
>
> So by this method we reach the conclusion that the living are generated from the dead, just as much as the dead from the living; and since this is the case, it seems a sufficient proof that the souls of the dead exist somewhere, whence they come back to life.

Could you really structure a business document like this?

Not in exactly this form; but the question and answer approach can be used to draw the reader along. For instance:

> Why are we gaining share at the low end?
>
> For two principal reasons: price and a product failure by our main competitor.
>
> How long will these advantages last?
>
> They're likely to cut price to match us within three months. The effect of the product failure may linger for a longer time.
>
> Can we do anything to maintain our enjoyment of these advantages as long as possible?
>
> Yes. There are three steps we can take. . . .

Telling the Reader What to Think

When we write to persuade, we try to channel the reader's thoughts from one point to another, without letting the reader know what's happening.

Sometimes you can expedite this channeling process by coming right out and planting the desired thought in the reader's mind with devices like the following:

> At this point you may be asking . . .
> Naturally you would anticipate . . .
> Let's try to impose some meaning on these figures . . .
> We can all see merit in both sides of this . . .

These channeling devices assume that the reader has certain questions on expectations. They do not assume the reader's *approval,* as in:

> You'll be interested to learn . . .

When channeling the reader's thoughts, avoid patting yourself on the back.

You can't put illogical thoughts in the reader's mind. Nor can you reverse a train of thought. These devices simply nudge them along paths they are already treading.

Spontaneous Interjections

A fairly long and detailed document outlines financing terms for proposed construction within one division of a company:

> At the closing, there was unanimous agreement on terms of three years at 11 percent. This accommodates Central Division's plans to avoid the insurance liability of a longer term.
> We are still waiting for a reading from Southeastern Division on terms for the Columbia project.
> Central Division expects ground to be broken by May 15 at the latest. . . .

The second paragraph of this sample—referring to Southeastern Division—has nothing to do with the subject of the document. The author of the document happened to think of the pending Southeastern business while in the course of transmitting this message on Central Division. Since the Southeastern situation is also of interest to the addressee, the author stuck it in and then went on with the mainstream of the message.

Now, this interpolation might cause only a momentary difficulty for the principal addressee, who will understand what's meant, sort it out, and go on reading. But others will be reading this document as well—and some of them may think that somehow the plans of the two divisions are interwoven, or indeed that Central's plans are contingent on Southeastern's. (They're not.)

When you're writing a message, and you're reminded of something that is only tangentially related, make a note—but don't stick it into the middle of the message. Save it for the end. Or, better yet, make a separate document out of it.

Half Empty or Half Full

It's time to make a progress report on your project, which is going reasonably well—not great, but not bad either. There is a temptation to see the glass as half full, and to indulge in self-back-patting.

Self-satisfaction when a project is progressing normally is a questionable tactic. You can chalk up a higher score by seeing the glass as half empty, expressing dissatisfaction with what hasn't gone right, and indicating your determination to do better:

As you can see, we are on track. These are days that might be seen as success. We don't see it that way. Although the odds are long, we're pushing to achieve better results than all of us envisioned. As a first step in that direction, next week we will kick off . . . [Here the writer describes a move that, while minor, has a good chance of working.]

Spin-Doctoring

The "spin doctor" is a recent political phenomenon. Spin doctors are operatives who try to influence media coverage of developments. After a debate between candidates, the spin doctors mingle with reporters, pointing out the triumphs of their own candidates and shortcomings of the opposing side.

The key to successful spin-doctoring is speed. The idea is to get your version of events out there first, before the other guy.

Take a leaf from the book of the spin doctors. When there is an important development, get out a fast message that puts a favorable spin on what has happened—that is, favorable to you. When a competing company announced an important new product, a manager spin-doctored the news this way:

WendelCo's entry into the high end of our market gives us an opportunity to respond at the lower end. We should be thinking about ways to exploit this development.

It happens that focus on the low end of the market would be favorable for the writer. Other managers will of course have different views. However, getting the "spin memo" out first helps to set the ground rules for the debate.

Covering Ignorance—Change the Subject

A manager is confronted with an alarming and puzzling memo:

Please explain the situation at Orizaba #2. Current information indicates that the operation is experiencing friction between Bench Assembly and Line Assembly re the production of HandiKits. Who is responsible for finished production? Respond ASAP.

Unfortunately the manager does not know, right at the moment, who's responsible. What should she do?

In such a situation, one useful tactic is to make an immediate response that changes the subject to something you *do* know about. This may buy you a little time to find out what's going on.

In this case, the manager replies:

The main question at Orizaba #2 is not who's responsible for finished production, but how we can establish smooth handoffs and cooperative relations between the units. One possibility is to . . .

The reply goes on to offer some substantial comments, which don't answer the question but which bear on the problem. Meanwhile the manager is getting a crash refresher on the doings at Orizaba #2.

Hedging a Forecast—Playing Lowball/Highball

When making a prediction, it's better—if possible—to forecast within a specified range than to forecast a specific result:

We will achieve a 7 percent reduction in CPU . . .
We will reduce CPU by 5–10 percent . . .

The first prediction makes the writer vulnerable because of its precision. Even if the reduction in cost per unit is greater than the forecast, the manager can be faulted for underestimation. When you go on record as predicting within a range, you cover yourself if the results are less than you expected, while you are in a position to take credit if the results are higher.

When you're talking, you can mention a precise figure, because your body language and subsequent comments can put the prediction in perspective. But when you commit a prediction to writing, you make yourself a hostage to fortune. Keep written forecasts within a range whenever possible. At first you may want to make the range very wide. When pressed for more precision, you can narrow it down, but still give yourself a decent margin.

Hedging a Prediction—Hang It on the Performance of Others

"I always avoid prophesying beforehand," said Winston Churchill, "because it is a much better policy to prophesy after the event has already taken place." Sound advice, not only for politicians, but also for those involved in building careers.

Sometimes, however, you're forced to go on record with a prediction. If you're right, you look good. If you're wrong, you look bad. So your optimum tactic is to make the prediction in such a way that you get the credit if it's accurate and avoid the blame (at least the full blame) if it turns out badly.

One way to accomplish this end is to key your prediction to exceptional performance of others:

> This expected increase in return on equity (ROE) is based on the following factors:
>
> - Continued growth in effectiveness of our aggressive strategy.
> - A reasonably healthy level of performance in the industry as a whole.
> - continued improvement in the effectiveness of field sales . . .

Putting the Other Person on the Spot

When people assure you that they'll do something, it's often a good idea to pin that assurance down in writing. Many assurances tend to be vague and slippery. Firm up that assurance in your response.

For example, a manager receives the following:

> You can be sure that we will devote our utmost attention to taking care of the problem by the last quarter at the latest . . .

The manager responds (with copies to the appropriate people):

> Thank you for your answer to my 6-618. You have committed yourself to a total restoration of standard functioning by September 30, if not earlier. I am delighted to receive this commitment.

Maybe the first writer did not intend the commitment to be all that firm. However, now it's necessary to accept the responsibility or try to weasel out of it.

Making an Evaluation—Lay Out the Ground Rules

When you make an evaluation of something, indicate at the beginning where you're coming from. Are you an expert? Were you given the assignment to make the evaluation? How exhaustive is your research or observation?

What kinds of criteria have you used? Your judgments will be most meaningful when they are placed in context:

> As you requested, I've looked over the Terrapin Research Complex. I spent three days at the complex and talked with the director, his two assistants, and the four project heads. Since my background is that of a line manager, not a scientist, I have evaluated the operation with regard to its organization, communications arrangements, management functioning, and cost control. . . .

Such a prospectus makes it clear that you are not pretending to qualifications that you don't possess. It enable readers to place the proper valuation on your judgments.

Routine Reports—Getting People to Read Them

Routine reports lose interest and readership. Obviously a recurrent report should be revised or dropped if people are not reading it. But in the real world, you may find yourself turning out documents that don't contain much that is likely to grab the intended readers.

It doesn't do any good to keep urging people to give the material their urgent attention. You become like the boy who cried "Wolf!" They'll just ignore even your important documents.

Admit that there are no bombshells in what you've written—and then tell your readers what they can expect and why they should at least glance at the material:

> This report covers events that you will find, by and large, to be familiar. As you go over it, I hope you'll look particularly for any signs that something might be going wrong, or ways we could do these things better.

Some work is routine. Admit it. Then remind readers that it's their job to review and react.

Warn Your Readers When the Going Gets Tough

Some subject matter resists all attempts to make it lighter and more interesting. It's technical or legal; it requires the use of long words and the digestion of difficult concepts. Maybe you could lighten it up if you really went all out, but you don't have time.

Tell readers that there's heavy going ahead. Don't apologize for it. Acknowledge that the material may not be fun, but it's important:

> The following sections describe in detail the principal aspects of the system and how it will function in various contingencies. You won't find it easy reading. Go through it carefully, stay with it until you understand it, and ask questions about anything you don't understand. It's difficult material, but you'll be accomplishing something very important by mastering it.

By preparing your readers for tough going ahead, you evoke the extra effort needed to comprehend the material, and you underscore the fact that most of what you write *is* easy to read.

Putting on the Pressure—The "Anguished" Question

In writing to pressure others for action, it's useful to take a leaf from the book of the experts who write collection letters.

One of the standard ploys of collection-letter writers is the "anguished" question:

> Would you really prefer us to resort to legal action? We would rather spare you, if possible, the hassle, emotional turmoil, and expense of a legal battle. We're used to them; we're good at them; we usually win them. I've seen what it does to those who try to oppose us. I want to spare you this.

The "would you really . . .?" approach says the writer is a good guy who has the power to do very bad things. And it says that if the reader persists in his misguided resistance, he will bring down the consequences on his own head.

At a key point in a pressure document, use the "anguished" question:

> Do you really want me to take this to the policy committee? I'd have to produce all the correspondence on this matter, and go into all the actions and decisions leading up to this impasse. . . .

Skip This Section If You're Just an Ordinary Writer

The lure of the forbidden—or even the things that are not intended for us—is age-old. When you tell readers they're not to read something, they're instantly curious about what's in there.

You're writing a report containing sections that vary in interest to different segments of the audience. Some people will read the parts that apply directly to them and skip the rest. You want people to read material that doesn't apply directly to them. You could exhort your audience:

> It's important to read every section of this report.

But you may have better luck if you play on the tendency to poke into places where we're not supposed to go. Label the sections you particularly want read:

Skip this section if you're not interested in the technology underlying our product changes, or if you're unable to understand it.

Your reader has to admit a deficiency if he skips the stuff. Your audience will pay particular attention to those "forbidden" sections.

Sedative Writing—When to Use the Passive Voice

All books on writing favor the active voice over the passive voice. Strunk and White (*The Elements of Style,* Third Edition, Macmillan, 1979, p. 18) say:

The active voice is usually more direct and vigorous than the passive:
   I shall always remember my first visit to Boston.
This is much better than:
   My first visit to Boston will always be remembered by me.

However, there are times when it's better not to be "direct and vigorous." For example, when criticizing someone's performance it's important to focus on fact rather than personality, so the passive voice may be more practical. Instead of "Your plan omitted a provision for alternative suppliers," you might say, "A plan for alternative suppliers was omitted from your plan."

Another time when calm should replace vigor is when the organization is grappling with a crisis. Nerves are raw. People are touchy. The language of communications ought to calm rather than excite:

The complete retrofit must be handled by your team before July 25.

This may not be good news to the reader, but it is less challenging (and potentially inflaming) than:

Your team must handle the complete retrofit before July 25.

Change of Pace—Revise the Standard Opening

Routine breeds neglect. After you've read a hundred documents that follow the same formula, it becomes difficult to give your full attention to the 101st.

To wake up your readers, make occasional changes in well-worn formats. For instance, the following executive summary treads a well-worn path:

Inorganic Coatings, Inc., has been in business for approximately eighteen months, and is presently headquartered in West Chester, Pennsylvania. The company manufactures and markets a NASA-patented inorganic zinc coating, named K-ZINC 531, which prevents steel corrosion.

Apart from the questionable use of "presently" (which means "in a little while" rather than "right now"), the opening is all right, but somewhat stale. The writer might change the opening to read:

A NASA-patented coating that prevents steel corrosion is the main product made and marketed by Inorganic Coatings, Inc., of West Chester, Pennsylvania. The company, in business eighteen months, calls the product K-ZINC 531.

Saying No While Offering Suggestions

When you say no you usually want to take some of the sting out of the negative. Flattery or vague promises won't do it. But you may be able to offer some practical help.

For example, a retailer writes to a large food distributor asking for a refund on an order. Here's the answer:

Since we have a long-standing policy of no returns or refunds on health-snack goods, I can't agree to your request.

Obviously you'd like to sell the goods rather than return them. So you may be interested in the success that Wardley's, in Branford, is having with the same line. Wardley's sells to a market area somewhat like yours. Here's what Wardley's is doing. . . .

The writer then provides details about the other store's successful approach. The recipient of the letter would still prefer to have gotten the refund, but practical information on what others are doing is always of interest.

You don't have to sugarcoat refusals. However, if you have some useful information, pass it along.

Business First, Apologies Later

Apologies and explanations in advance of the message are annoying and wasteful:

I'm sorry to have to send you the following report. As you're well aware, the budget process is a series of decisions that have to balance with each other and with the overall objectives of the organization. A number of proposals of considerable merit were on the table this year. . . .

By this time the reader knows it's bad news, but he's fuming until the writer gets to the point. Actually, most readers skip such an introduction to reach the guts of the document.

Give the message right away. Then provide an explanation, but don't go overboard in trying to apologize:

Your request for $750,000 for plant modernization during FY 92 has not been approved.
There is considerable merit to the proposal.
The timing is wrong. . . .

Setting an Informal Tone

Contact (or call) reports cover contacts even when not much happens during the contact. With a brief, informal note you can convey the flavor of the contact.

Spoke with Joe McCarran of MonMar on 7/2/91 about MonMar's proposed move into Cincinnati. Joe feels Cincinnati is "a great area for expansion." While available funding is always important in such a move, he feels money is not necessarily the controlling factor. But he added that MonMar is not ready to talk about a timetable.

This reflects the not-overly-important nature of the exchange. It also conveys, without spelling it out, that the author is not holding her breath until MonMar actually makes the move that is being discussed.

Avoid Accusations

To: All Department Members
Re: Use of Departmental Fax Machines

It has come to my attention that some employees are using departmental fax machines for personal messages. More importantly, excessive use of fax for outgoing routine messages makes the fax machines unavailable for incoming traffic. Therefore, it's important to observe the following guidelines about use of fax. . . .

Once you get past the first sentence of this memo, you realize that it is an attempt to solve a substantive problem—the clogging of incoming channels because of the faxing of *legitimate,* though routine, messages. The bit about personal use is not the main point at all. But when the accusation leads the memo, it has a distinctly negative effect on the way the message is received. Those who have not been using the fax for personal stuff are insulted or amused. They don't feel the message applies to them.

General accusations should always be avoided. They are especially bad when they detract from a more substantial message. This memo should have started:

In order to free up our fax machines for important incoming traffic, it's necessary to observe some guidelines about outgoing messages. . . .

Tough but Informal Openings

You want to get tough—but you want to keep the atmosphere cool enough so that the other party is neither too angry nor too resentful to perform effectively. When you're talking face to face it's easier to maintain a loose atmosphere because you can see the other person's reactions and adjust accordingly.

In writing it's more difficult. However, when you want to be tough and cordial at the same time, avoid heavy-handed formality:

Your detailed plan for execution of my directive of 6/16 was due at this office by close of business yesterday, 6/23. Since you have not forwarded the plan, I can only conclude . . .

Instead, try something more informal:

Did I miss something? Your plan was supposed to be here by now. Evidently you're having trouble. What's the problem? Let me know right away. Maybe there's something I can do. Because we *have* to have your plan right away.

Keep "You" out of a Negative Context

You're writing to inform a supplier of a mistake in a shipment:

Shipment #16E/714, received on 4/16, is incorrect in the following respects:
 1,200 of the tips are fitted with 3/8″ bits rather than 1/2″ bits.
 There are 4,600 #4 insertion keys; the order calls for 4,300.
 There are 3,700 #5 insertion keys; the order calls for 4,000.
I know you will make the necessary corrections immediately.

That's a good way to do it because it is *impersonal*. Contrast it with this:

You shipped us a most incorrect order. We ordered 4,300 #4 insertion keys. You sent us 4,600. You sent us 3,700 #5 insertion keys when we ordered 4,000. And on 1,200 of the tips you should have used 1/2″ bits. . . .

When a mistake has been made, gratuitous use of "you" seems aggressive and accusatory. Even if the whole thing is the personal fault of the person being addressed, you're primarily interested in getting it straightened out, not in scoring points. So use an impersonal style that reduces the heat.

When Variety Is Not the Spice of Life

You can stretch too far in trying to inject variety into a document. Take the following:

At our Paterson plant, they use a chromium dip tank. An electroplating process is employed at our Camden facility, while at the Scranton location a metal-veneering procedure is implemented.

The writer sets great store by variety and, in striving for it, avoids repetition. This results in a series of synonyms (or near-synonyms): *use, employ, implement, plant, facility, location.*

This is needless variety. It seems indecisive. The paragraph is stronger and clearer when key words are repeated—or left out. (Why keep looking for alternatives to "factory"?)

At our Paterson plant they use a chromium dip tank. In Camden they use electroplating. In Scranton they use metal veneering.

The point of the passage is that a number of different ways are used to achieve approximately the same effect. Therefore the paragraph would benefit from repetition of the verb "use."

Here's another effort to avoid repetition:

Chemical analysis of the water indicates that the double filtration unit reduces chlorine content an average of 23 percent. Results of the appraisal should be reflected in new sales literature. Inform field representatives of the assessment.

The writer uses "appraisal" and "assessment" to keep from saying "analysis" again. But the substitute words weaken and confuse the message. "Appraisal" is less precise than "analysis," and "assessment" is so much broader and vaguer that the recipient may well be confused about the meaning. Does the writer want field representatives to be told about the results of the chemical analysis or about the judgment that the figures will be used in sales literature?

When the word is right, don't worry about finding a substitute:

Chemical analysis of the water indicates that the double filtration unit reduces chlorine an average of 23 percent. Analysis results should be reflected in new sales literature. Inform field representatives of the analysis results.

When you find yourself straining for another word in order to avoid repetition, stop. If the repetition is clearer and simpler, use it.

Dot-Dot-Dot . . . The Deliberate Incompletion . . .

In speech we sometimes use—and hear others use—a kind of deliberate incompletion, in which the voice trails off as a sentence is left unfinished. The effect is to leave a suggestion (or an insinuation) in the air without actually uttering it:

"I wonder if he really means that . . ."
"The check is in the mail . . ."
"Sure I believe you, but . . ."

Writer use three dots (or leaders) to indicate this trailing off of the voice.

Business writing deals in *definites*. There is little room for the calculated ambiguity denoted by the dots. But every once in a while you may achieve an interesting effect by using this device. Say, for example, a supplier has promised delivery by a certain date. You want to indicate that you're hopeful but skeptical—that the jury is still out, and that you'll believe it when you see it. You don't want to put that down on paper. So you write:

I'm pleased that you're going to be able to complete delivery by 6/16. That's good news in the light of previous experience. We'll be waiting . . .

Gambit—Giving Something to Get Something

In chess, a gambit is the offering of a piece to your opponent so that you can gain an advantage. When you're writing to get somebody to do something, you may increase the persuasive power of the message by offering a gambit up front:

For six months our departments have been at odds over responsibility for maintenance of the relay station.
　　We are willing to assume this responsibility. In return we ask that you . . .

But putting the enticing "gambit" at the beginning, you encourage the addressee to read your proposition in a favorable context.

Answering the Unasked Question

A senior manager has posed two specific questions:

Has the new advertising agency been thoroughly briefed on the company's merchandising philosophy?
When will the agency's first concepts be submitted?

The manager to whom these questions have been directed responds with the facts. But the manager doesn't stop there. He adds:

The agency has assigned a first-class creative team to our business. Bob Wilson, the group head, has won three Cleos and has handled clients in our industry. Bob and his group are working very closely with us. They welcome our input . . .

Who asked? Why is the manager passing along uncalled-for comments?

Because the manager perceived an *unasked question* in the senior manager's request. The overt questions, in the responding manager's view, signal an uneasiness about whether the new agency is taking the company's needs seriously enough. So the manager answers the real question.

When you feel that a question has not been asked (but is nonetheless in the air), answer it. (Of course it helps if you have a good answer.) It demonstrates your perceptiveness, and it fulfills the true purpose of communication.

Less Is More—The Art of Leaving Things Out

A proposal ends with these two sentences:

We are well qualified to handle this assignment. We have the expertise and the track record.

This is a punchy, effective windup. Compare it with this:

It is our conviction that we are well-qualified to handle this assignment, due to the fact that we have the expertise and the track record that demonstrate our capacity to meet the requirements set forth in the project description.

Sometimes excess words are the equivalent of throat clearing. A speaker, not knowing exactly what to say, stalls by using flabby verbiage. Once those words are said they can't be unsaid. The writer has the advantage of being able to remove the flab.

When you're seeking the best way to say something, doodle on a pad or just think. Don't write sentences until you're sure they're free of unnecessary weight.

What you leave out gives more impact to what you leave in.

More on What to Leave Out

Here's a passage from a planning document:

In gauging allocation of corporate resources among wholly owned bottlers, Finance/Planning must measure how much of the bottler's effort goes into overall brand promotion as compared with location-specific promotions. In approaching this question . . .

Here's how the writer revised it:

How much of the bottler's effort goes into overall brand promotion as compared with location-specific promotions? In approaching this question . . .

Ellipsis—leaving things out—is a useful tool for professional writers. Put yourself in the reader's place when you look at your document. Apply the "of course" test. Anything the reader can infer ("Of course that's what it means"), leave out.

You'll have a cleaner, faster piece of writing.

Wearing a Belt and Suspenders

The president of a strategic business unit wants a divisional vice-president to brief key people on a new Management Information Service (MIS) policy:

The new setup goes into effect March 17. Please alert your group.

Fine. Actually the second sentence is almost surely unnecessary. But if it ended there, it would be okay. Unfortunately the president goes on:

The best procedure would be to call a meeting around the 12th. This gives you time to hold face-to-face discussions. Send an announcement memo to all concerned right after the meeting, and a brief reminder on the 16th . . .

The president doesn't really think the vice-president doesn't know enough to call a meeting, send a memo, and all the rest of it. (If that were the case it would be a lot more than a writing problem.)

No. The president is one of those people who tend to go into unneeded detail when they write. They don't do it when they're talking—they're sure the other party gets the point. But in communicating by writing they feel less secure. So they make sure, to the extend of redundancy and perhaps insult. The recipient might well say, "Does this guy think he has to tie my shoe-laces?"

Be secure enough in your writing that you know when to stop.

Make Up a Quotation to Make a Point

The talkative taxi driver used to be a cliché of journalism. Whenever a foreign correspondent sent an "overview" story, the piece would begin with a snappy quote from a taxi driver. The quote always fitted right in with the tone the reporter wanted to set and the points the reporter wanted to make. Needless to say, the quotes (if not the taxi drivers) were almost always invented.

The device can be used to convey an attitude or sum up a point in a document. For example:

As sales have declined, tension has increased and the spread of rumors has accelerated. People in the division are worried about what they see to be imminent cutbacks. One individual remarked to me, "When I come in in the morning, I never know if I'll still have a job by the end of the day."

Maybe that was actually said, in just those words; maybe not. It doesn't matter. The reader isn't going to question it; and the quote reinforces the impression the writer wants to convey.

Overstatement for Acceptance of a New Thought

You're about to propose something that will startle—maybe even shock—the reader. You want the reader to read through to the end and consider your proposal with at least some degree of objectivity. The danger is that the other party will be so shaken up by your opening paragraphs that the memo will be crumpled up and thrown in the wastebasket before the end is reached.

Condition your reader at the beginning with an overstatement:

You're going to be outraged by this proposal. It will test to the limit your powers of objectivity. I ask you to read it through and try to consider it fairly in spite of your gut reaction.

Use a Neutral Opening to Get Objective Opinions

The CEO of a credit card company opened an important message to his key people with the following words:

The attached research shows that we are in danger of becoming known as the "blue-collar" card. Please give me your thoughts on this ASAP.

One of the addressees had, indeed, been thinking about the fact that the card was not perceived as being for the very top stratum of the market. She did not necessarily think it was a bad thing. In fact, she had been beginning to sketch out a campaign to take advantage of this perception.

But when the boss said, "We are *in danger* of becoming known as the 'blue-collar' card," he signaled clearly his feeling that this was a very bad thing. So all the responses made suggestions about how to reverse the trend. It took another year and millions in unsuccessful advertising before the company stopped trying to stave off the dreaded "blue-collar" designation and decided to go with the flow, selling aggressively into the niche market.

This decision could have been made a lot earlier if the CEO had invited open discussion, rather than influencing the response by tipping his own feelings.

A better opening would have been:

The attached research shows that we are tending toward being regarded as the "blue-collar" card. Your thoughts on this development, please.

When you want to elicit unbiased response, make your invitation altogether neutral.

Using Analogy to Make a Point

Elsewhere in this book we used an example of a memo intended to persuade people to complete the composition of documents before connecting to E-mail. (This, incidentally, is a good habit for anyone who uses electronic mail services.)

Here's a case where you can drive the point home with an analogy:

Let's compose and store before uploading—We all agree that it would be pretty wasteful to put through a call to Hong Kong before thinking of what we wanted to say. In the same way it's wasteful to connect to E-mail before we're ready to transmit. As soon as you make the connection the meter starts to run. Please compose and edit first, then upload.

Colorful Comparisons

"She came on like Gangbusters."
"I need this like a moose needs a hatrack."
"You're as pale as a ghost."

Similes are among the most common figures of speech. You make your point vividly by comparing two unlikely things. We use similes so often in speaking that they become clichés.

But we tend to limit such colorful uses of words to talk. When we write business documents we tend to be serious to the point of solemnity. With good reason. If you stick a lot of fancy writing into a formal report, people may think you're a flake, even if you write very well.

Once in a while, however, you can achieve a striking effect through the adroit use of an apt figure of speech. Here, for example, the writer wants to emphasize the point that the company's leading competitor will react strongly to the threat of a new product line:

Their tendency will be to defend their leadership position by using all available resources.

The writer might try this:

They'll fight like tigers to defend their market share.

It's a crisp, conversational way of making the point. A rhetorician would point out that ''fight like tigers'' is trite. True. If you were writing a short story you'd want to use fresher imagery.

But not in a business document. The familiar figure of speech adds color but doesn't call attention to itself.

Let yourself go once in a while. Use a simile.

CHAPTER 5

Velocity and Impact

Professional writers use certain techniques to keep their copy moving and, at intervals, hit the reader between the eyes. Velocity and impact techniques are as important in business documents as they are in romance novels or spy thrillers. Here's a sampling of such methods. Used in the right places, they can give extra life to an ordinary document.

Impact and Image

Every important document you write should do two things:

- Convey to the reader exactly what you want to convey—that's *impact*.
- Present you in an advantageous light—that's *image*.

Impact is necessary to getting the job done. Image is necessary to winning favorable visibility and achieving your career goals. So-so writing is not enough to achieve either. Today, more than ever, your writing skill must be on a par with your ability to think and talk.

Writing is the delivery system of power. As you climb the ladder, you are called upon to exert authority over longer reaches. Mediocre writing drains away your power, dims the light of your creativity, muddies the clear waters of your thought.

You should feel just as comfortable and self-confident when you write as when you talk. If the act of writing well seems difficult, it *is* difficult, more difficult than necessary. The prophecy fulfills itself. If you have to think too much about writing, you write timidly. Uncertainty in writing is as bad as uncertainty in any other area of the managerial art.

Not every document has to be a masterpiece. But every document should have punch, clarity, and cohesion. And certain key documents should be written with all the style and flair you can muster.

Writing is a tool. It is also a weapon. Business is often combat—with competing companies and with rivals whom you have to beat to get the biggest money and the best jobs.

In this chapter you will find a catalog of strategies, tactics, ploys, and putdowns that you can use in the fascinating but dangerous game of company politics. You might call it the Dirty Tricks Department.

Hard-Hitting Openings

''Call me Ishmael.''

Herman Melville's three-word opening of *Moby Dick* is one of the most famous first sentences in literature: blunt, conversational, somewhat aggressive.

Business documents are not the Great American Novel. They're fact, not fiction—or at least we hope they are. Nevertheless, a terse opening can do a lot to give urgency and character to a document.

For example, a manager is about to present recommendations for a restructuring. The details may be somewhat dull, but the subject is important. The manager begins:

We've got to get organized.

Some other blunt openings:

September 15 is a pivotal date.
The ball is in our court.
First, the bad news.
We have one more chance, and this time we'll win.

The unusual, punchy opening must be used only with highly important messages. It signals that *this is urgent*. Because it is a departure from the conventions, it must never be followed by trivialities. And it can't be used frequently.

In the right spot, however, a short, conversational opening sentence can enhance the impact of your message.

Start with a Grabber

At work and at home, you're besieged by direct mail. Most of it goes right into the wastebasket. But it's worth looking at—not necessarily to buy the products, but because the direct mail writers use some tricks that can be useful to the business document writer.

For example, here's the start of a direct mail appeal written for Western Union. The object is to persuade travel agents to use Western Union services like Mailgram, Priority Letter, and Custom Letter. The personalized appeal (sent via Western Union) starts:

Dear ———

Are you still trusting your important messages to ordinary mail?

While this may not be an award winner, it typifies some of the techniques of the direct mail writer, who must command attention instantly. It's a question, and well-chosen questions tend to elicit answers. It implies that the addressee may be doing something outdated and, perhaps, dangerous. It sets up the pitch by casting doubt on the status quo.

Now let's take a look at a persuasion memo written by a manager. It begins:

This is to examine our present methods of distribution of counter goods to convenience stores in the northeast.

The writer, who has a case to make, could take a tip from the direct mail folks and begin like this:

Why are we still shipping counter goods by truck over 400-mile routes?

Start with an Exclamation

That's more like it!
We're on a roll!
Here's some good news!
Great!

You want to jolt your readers, make them eager to get your message. It's not a formal, routine report, nor a memo that should follow a previously established pattern. You're writing something a little different.

Wake up the reader's eye with an exclamation. You set a conversational tone. You convey human feeling. And you establish the frame of reference within which you want the reader to receive the message.

Lead with the News—Not What Everybody Knows

Here are two possible leads:

Japanese cars have achieved a substantial share of the U.S. market. American consumers perceive Japanese automobiles as well made. We may be able to capitalize on these trends by bringing out a line keyed specifically to Japanese imports.

We may be able to capitalize on the success of Japanese cars in the United States by bringing out a line keyed specifically to these Japanese imports.

The first lead features what everybody knows. The second starts with the new idea. The second approach works better. It's true that new ideas should be placed in context. But when the context is obvious, it's not necessary to emphasize it.

Get to the Meat Faster

Eliminate needless introductory words—unless you have a specific reason to delay getting to the meat. Some introductory words become habitual:

Due to the fact that there is a question as to whether or not we should increase our offshore activity, we should defer this decision for a month.

"Due to" . . . "the fact that" . . . "question as to whether or not"—verbal tics like these are annoying when spoken, harmful when written. Cut them out:

Because there is a question about increasing our offshore activity, we should defer this decision for a month.

Give the Bad (or Good) News First

A memo begins:

On December 16 you submitted a request for a supplemental appropriation to cover reorganization of the feeder lines in Location 3. We have given careful consideration to the points you raised . . .

The memo goes on for several paragraphs, weighing the pros and cons. Then:

On the basis of these factors, we have decided not to approve the supplemental at this time . . .

Of course the recipient of this message will have skipped over all the preliminary stuff to get to the decision.

Don't make it necessary for your audience to hunt for the most important news, especially if it's bad news. "Let's cut to the chase," as they say. Make the announcement up front:

We have decided not to approve the supplemental you requested.
Here are the factors we considered in reaching this decision . . .

Identify the Cast of Characters

A memo begins:

George and I met with Harvey and Marie at lunch. We explored several aspects of their current situation and next year's plans for expansion . . .

The memo goes on to give a clear description of the subjects mentioned. To some readers, it's quite satisfactory. But a senior executive—one step removed from the scene—starts to read the document and asks, "Who are Harvey and Marie?" These people are never identified, because the writer assumed they were well-known to all those who would read the memo.

Make it standard procedure to assume that your messages—at least those of some substance—will be read by people who are not familiar with every detail. Use common sense—when sending a brief update note to somebody with whom you are in daily contact, it is probably unnecessary to give the entire history of the subject. But when there's even a chance that what you write may be of interest to a wider circle, include the relevant background.

Remember that your more important documents may be reviewed later by executives who just want an overview or even by people who are evaluating your work. With this thought in mind, the above memo might better have started:

George Walker and I met with Harvey Ganz and Marie Dunnigan, president and VP marketing of Cobalt Minerals, at lunch . . .

As you write, imagine that the CEO of your company, who has not followed the situation, will be reading your words. Are they clear enough for him or her?

Throat Clearing

The memo begins:

This is to respond to your fax (yesterday, June 21, 1990) requesting clarification of previous communications relating to time frames for national distribution on Lime-Bomb and insertion of Lime-Bomb Lite into test phase II . . .

The request came the previous day. The introduction is too wordy. Get to it faster:

Re your query on Lime-Bomb and Lime-Bomb Lite phase II—we plan national distribution . . .

Sometimes when we talk, we preface the important message with the verbal equivalent of throat clearing. We do this to alert the listener that a message is on the way. When we think the listener's channels are open, we proceed with the important stuff.

That's not necessary in writing. Say enough up front to tell the reader what it's about. Then get to the point.

Action Upgrading

Vitalize your writing by upgrading verbs to get brighter color, quicker movement, harder hitting.

The first verb you think of may be lackluster:

The project is <u>progressing</u> on schedule.

We can do better than "progressing," which is about as unpictorial a word for movement as you can get. Let's try a two-minute workout. We will ask some questions about the project that is "progressing." The idea is to compare it to something that moves.

> If the project had wheels, what would it be like? A car? What kind? Big or small? Luxury car? Sports car? Economy car? Limo? Pickup?
> How does it move? Roll? Zip? Parade? Zigzag? Cruise?
> Or is the project bigger? A truck? Bulldozer? Tank?

Maybe the project resembles a tank. Strong, massive, aggressive, designed to demolish competition. Okay. Tanks don't just "progress." What do they do?

The project is <u>rumbling</u> along on schedule.

In this case the verb "rumbling" gives a look and a sound to the description of what the project is doing. "Rumbling" conveys the idea that the forward movement is steady and powerful, but not without clunks and squeaks along the way.

To upgrade a verb, here's a three-step plan:

Say it. When you talk you probably don't use the kind of stilted words that tend to creep into writing. When you're on the verge of writing a verb like "progressing," say out loud what you mean. You'll probably come up with a better word. Write it, even if it sounds too slangy or down-to-earth.

Compare it. Find an analogy. An activity. A sport. A sickness. Song, movie, play. Whatever. Toys, games, household chores. Hobbies. Look for the action or the thing that can be seen, or heard, or felt.

Check it in the thesaurus. Your thesaurus in dictionary form lets you browse through a boutique of verbs, hefting them, handling them, trying them out. Let's say the concept you want to express is ''increase.'' You can use ''increase'' as a verb, but maybe there's something better. A glance in the thesaurus will give you a choice among words like *boost, multiply, grow, surge, expand, amplify,* and the like. Somewhere in there is a word that gets across the idea of ''increase'' with brilliance and punch.

Abstract verbs require processing by the intellect before they become ideas. Action verbs pierce right to the core of consciousness, planting an instant image in the reader's mind. Action verbs are the firepower of your prose, giving your ideas reach and penetration. Good thoughts deserve effective delivery. Don't lob your ideas; fire them to the target with a verb that makes the reader see and imagine, not just think.

Verbing for Fun and Impact

Some purists are scandalized at the practice of making verbs out of nouns—Xeroxed, in-boxed, faxed, and so on. Writing consultant Paula Ludlow tells audiences about a manager who says, ''I'll try to window you in for lunch next week.''

True, ''verbing'' (this author's invented term for turning nouns into verbs) can be carried to extremes (or ''extremed''). But English is a living language, and part of its evolution is the creation of new verbs out of new nouns, or out of old nouns that take on a new meaning. ''Stonewall,'' for example, is a synthesized verb that expresses its meaning better than any other verb would do.

So there's nothing wrong with ''windowing.'' The term ''window of opportunity,'' popularized by reports of NASA launches, denotes an opening that will close unless it is taken advantage of in time. When a noun/verb best expresses your meaning, use it. However, if it's a very new coinage, one that is used by a small group or a particular organization, make sure all your readers know what it means.

What you have just read is heresy. The idea of making up verbs, well, it absolutely scandalizes traditionalists. They're especially appalled if such outrages are recommended for business documents.

We've had too much traditionalism. It's time to break free. It's time to start *verbing*.

Verbing is a great exercise. It kicks in your creative lobes and loosens up your writing muscles. Verbing is the creation of new verbs. Business is a fountainhead of new verbs. Who first said, "Fax it"? Or, "I'll Fedex it to you"? Or, "Please Xerox this for me"? The names of these gifted verbers are unknown, but their creations live on.

But "verb" is often treated like a four-letter word. Instead of trying for the most vivid action words, business writers dull the impact. They achieve dullness by choosing the passive voice:

The project will be undertaken by us.

Getting the most out of verbs starts with the active voice:

We will undertake the project.

But there's more to it than that. Some verbs, like "undertake," boast little in the way of thrills, except maybe to an undertaker. Other verbs hit the reader's mind with images and movement:

We will handle the project.
We will control the project.
We've seized the project.
We're going to muscle this project through.

Different verbs for different meanings, and also for different degrees of impact.

If there is color and movement in your thoughts, there must be color and movement in your language. Find the most vivid verbs you can find. If existing verbs are not vivid enough, *make up new ones.*

Verbs are where the action is. Verbs are the action words, giving impetus and impact to what we say and write.

New verbs are constantly coming into the language to describe the new things we do. Many verbs evolve through the actionizing of nouns. It's a natural process. One day my son, asked what his father was doing at the moment, replied, "Daddy is desking." *Desking*—his made-up word—is an ideal verb to describe the things we do at a desk—straightening out the papers, arranging the in-box, sharpening the pencils, and so on.

Ignore those who bemoan the making up of verbs. When you have a chance to verb your copy into more vivid life, *verb away!*

One category of created verb is the compound:

We're trying to high-end the line.
Bottom-line that for me.
Let's back-burner this issue for a while.

Another verbing technique: add an action ending like "ize" or "ate." Some verbers add an action ending when they don't have to:

Our objective is to mainstreamize the product three months after completion of the tests.

The "ize" is superfluous: "mainstream" works better as a verb in this sentence. The best use of the action ending may be the creation of a verb that has meaning only within the organization. "Have these candidates been Armonkized?" means—to insiders—"Have these candidates gone through the training course given in Armonk?" You can make verbs out of people's names: "To reduce the risk, we should Marvinize that equipment." Meaningless to the uninitiated, but to the reader of this message, "Marvinize" means enlist the services of a company technical specialist named Marvin. Try to create verbs without using a hyphen: "agendize" is better than "agenda-ize."

Some verbers create combo-verbs with the word "out"—scope out, concept out.

The purest form of verbing coins single-word verbs out of nouns:

It will cost less to redesign the product than to glitz it.
You'll have to flurry this project through.
These numbers don't mean much until they've been goaled.

Verbing is good exercise. You can do it anytime, anywhere. While sitting through a boring meeting, let your mind play at the game of creating verbs. You won't use all the products of your verbing in actual messages, not by a damn sight. For one thing, you have to be sure of your readers. An up-tight addressee, brainwashed by the purists, may think you're some kind of verbal bolshevik.

But in the right situation, created verbs power your prose to maximum impact.

Using the "Menu" Approach to Get Action

People don't like to be told what to do. They want to be free to make their own choices. However, managers often have to give orders that allow little leeway.

There's a way to tell people what to do, and give them a choice at the same time. Here's an example. The writer has laid out a course of action to be followed. The memo concludes:

Being close to the situation, you're the best judge of how to proceed. There are a number of ways the program could be kicked off:

- general announcement to all dealers
- one-on-one meetings with high-volume dealers
- telephone notification from HQ
- press release to the trades

Let me know what you decide.

The "menu" presented by the writer offers choices within a fairly narrow range. The point is that the program is going to be instituted, no matter what the subordinate thinks. However, the menu approach lets the subordinate make choices and maintain, at least to some degree, a feeling of autonomy.

Shocking Language

Every now and then you can use shocking language with great impact and usefulness. For example, here's one way that a writer might express the reaction of a customer to the company's explanations:

I told Edwards that the problem had been corrected and that he could be sure deliveries would be timely and accurate from now on. He expressed skepticism.

Here's another way:

I told Edwards that the problem had been corrected and that he could be sure deliveries would be timely and accurate from now on. To this he said, "Bullshit!"

The brutally profane response is unbusinesslike, but it conveys the cynical disbelief of the customer and the extent of the company's credibility problem. Profanity has no regular place in business writing. However, there are times when it says what you want to say far better than any other words. When that's the case, go with it.

"We Do Not Lie"

It's a good idea to avoid expressions like "honestly" and "to tell the truth" because they seem insincere. Assertions of personal integrity can have an unfortunate ring, sort of like Richard Nixon's celebrated statement that "I am not a crook!"

However, when you use it in the right place, the assurance of personal honesty can be quite effective. Take, for example, the following excerpts from a letter written by John E. Pepper, president of Procter & Gamble, printed in *The Wall Street Journal* on July 27, 1990. Mr. Pepper is disputing a *Journal* story that said he had interviewed for the Campbell Soup CEO job:

We told [the WSJ reporter] the reports she had received were "flat wrong." I didn't have one conversation or one contact about the Campbell position with anyone. Moreover, we confirmed this in writing.

> Your staff knows our company. <u>We do not lie.</u> At a minimum I would have
> expected, with this flat denial, a professional job . . .

We do not lie. That direct assertion is very effective in supporting the
particular point, and also in projecting the integrity of the writer and the
organization.

Such an assertion can have great impact in the right place. Of course it has
to be credible. A manager with an extensive reputation for trickiness and
dishonesty can't get away with it. But when you have an important point to
make, consider putting in the personal assertion of truth:

> We will continue to back this project up with all available resources. You know
> me. You know you can count on the truth of that statement.

The personal assertion of truth works only when it's used sparingly, and
used on matters of importance. When these conditions are met, it can have
real impact.

Making Extreme Statements for Effect

Exaggeration for effect is a commonplace of colorful speech:

> "He tore his hair out!"
> "The Broncos trampled all over the Rams."
> "Everybody must be absolutely crazy over there!"
> "I could eat a horse."

Hyperbole—exaggeration for effect—works when we're talking with
somebody because our tone of voice, expressions, and gestures—along with
the trite nature of the words—make it clear that the statement is not to be taken
literally.

Exaggeration in writing is tricky. Familiar hyperbolic expressions look
stale:

> They couldn't care less.
> It's cheap at any price.

There are times when you can achieve impact through exaggeration.
Positive exaggeration works better than negative exaggeration. When a senior
manager writes, "Merchandising must be out of their minds to suggest this,"
he is pretty sure to offend at least some of the people in Merchandising. But
people don't get mad at positive exaggeration:

> Your idea will sweep the country.

Exaggerate to praise, not to criticize.

Keeping Up the Momentum

There should be a good reason for sending any message. Usually that good reason is implicit in the content of the message. But here's a note that doesn't seem to have any content in the usual sense:

> I read your latest report with great interest. The figures on population growth in the target area are significant. It's good to see that you're on course and moving . . .

This is a "momentum note." It doesn't carry anything fresh in the way of information, but it conveys a sense of involvement and encouragement. (And it says, "I'm reading the mail I get from you.")

When a relationship involves continuing exchanges, stick in a momentum note here and there to change the pace and assure the other party that the effort is worthwhile.

Transition Words

"Proceeding Logically"

When the logic of a document's organization is crystal-clear, you don't have to call attention to it. But sometimes the organization is not all that clear.

For example, let's say you want to give a certain point greater importance than it has been given in previous discussions of the topic. You could write an explanation:

> Not enough attention has been paid to the importance of fully trained customer relations people in the success of this campaign. In a great number of cases, customer satisfaction is eroded . . .

And so on. But this sort of argument can be contentious and break the flow of the message. Instead, emphasize the importance of the point by moving it to a prominent place in the document and underscoring the fact that your positioning is no accident:

> Proceeding logically, we come next to customer relations . . .

"Next in Importance"

You are making several points in a memo. You arrange the points in their order of importance, with the most important first. However, some of the subordinate points require a lot more space than the most important points. So, on the page, the unequal length may give a misleading impression about the relative significance of the sections.

Give the reader a clue by introducing the subordinate, although lengthy, paragraph with words that assign the proper weight:

Next in importance is the redesign of the casing. Beginning with the lateral dimensions . . .

Such transitions move readers along and also give them subtle—sometimes almost subliminal—nudges that condition their thinking about what they'll read next.

"Along the Same Lines"

William Strunk, Jr., and E. B. White (*The Elements of Style,* third edition, Macmillan, 1979, p. 52) comment that the term "along these lines" has been so overworked "that a writer who aims at freshness or originality had better discard it entirely."

Hey, not so fast! Writers of business documents aim at *effect*. Though freshness and originality are often essential in achieving the desired effect, familiar phrases have their uses as well. "Along the same lines" and allied expressions are practically invisible direction signals that guide the reader. The words show, obviously, that what follows is in the same category as the material that preceded it:

Along the same lines, we will be spotlighting the price differential in selling to convenience stores . . .

Echoing the Last Point

New paragraphs introduce new thoughts. But when a paragraph makes an abrupt change from the previous paragraph, the effect is disconnected and jerky.

You can achieve continuity and a sense of fluid transition by echoing words from the last part of the preceding paragraph:

Group mailing is particularly useful in sending urgent messages to regional executives. Through the messaging feature, the executive list can be segmented in various ways. The appropriate list or combination of lists is selected. One message is then created and automatically transmitted (to each executive's mailbox, fax, etc.). Support for group transmission expedites the messaging process by automating designation of select groups.
   Among the designated select groups, the urgency of messages can vary. The system provides multiple delivery options . . .

If the second paragraph had begun, "The urgency of messages can vary," there would have been a slight but perceptible jog in continuity. Keep the message flowing by echoing previous points.

Change Direction with "However"

You're commenting on a proposal. Your comments are generally favorable. You expand some parts and change some details.

But you've got a few reservations about the proposal. They are not major disagreements. Nevertheless, you want to get them on the record without looking as if you're too negative.

The word "however" is a valuable transition word in this situation:

The plan is a good one. However, it's important to raise a couple of cautions . . .

This usage calls attention to the reservations without making an overly big deal of them. It's better than saying something more formal and ominous:

At this point it is necessary to call attention to certain cautions . . .

Use Questions to Keep the Reader on Track

Periodic questions inserted into a complex document can keep the reader on track and prepare the reader for what is to come next.

Here's how the device is used in a twelve-page document covering the details of a change in marketing strategy:

Why switch from single-line schedules to market franchising?
Under the old system we made no attempt to match our franchises with the distributor's sales pattern. Most wholesalers identify the market segments they can serve most profitably . . . [The paragraph continues at some length. Then the writer uses another question:]

How do we sell market franchising to distributors?
Every distributor looks for three things from manufacturers: brand acceptance, service, profitability . . .

The questions you used in structuring the document can sometimes work well as actual elements of the document.

Build Urgency into Your Style

You get a message that starts like this:

Recent figures show that the Western Area is lagging behind the rest of the country in a number of important respects. Volume has fallen short of quota for four months, and last month showed an actual decline against last year. In addition, we are seeing a sharper increase in the ratio of calls to sales than we've seen in the past, while at the same time total number of calls has not exceeded last year, in spite of the fact that one of our targets was a 20 percent increase in calls . . .

The words are clear enough, but the *pace* does not reflect the urgency that the writer wants to convey. When you want to say, *"This is urgent!"* use short bursts in a staccato style:

Western is lagging badly. Volume short of quota for four months. Last month actually down from a year ago. Calls/sales ratio up sharply. Total calls are flat . . .

When to Be Negative

Should you try to make everything positive? Some business writers say yes. Instead of a negative wording:

They made the wrong decision in Birmingham.

They try for the positive:

They did not arrive at the best possible decision in Birmingham.

Don't bend over backwards to avoid being negative, when negativity is the essence of your message. The Ten Commandments are negative injunctions, and they have stood up pretty well. "Thou shalt not kill" works better than "Try to find some alternative to killing."

So when your message is *no*, say *no*:

Stop offering 60-day terms at once.
Do not fax any part of this plan without my authorization.
No more B-70s will be issued until further notice.

Pulling Rank

Authoritarianism hasn't gone out of fashion altogether, but it's not the dominant mode of the day. We tend to like a more democratic management style, in which the chain of command is always implicit, but which encourages free exchange of ideas and opinions up and down the ladder.

Now and then it's necessary to remind subordinates that you outrank them. This is true, for example, in cases where there has been spirited debate over a policy, leading to your making a decision. Now you want the arguments to stop, but you can't just switch people off. When you encourage a flow of ideas, that flow may continue past the point at which you'd like it to cease.

It's awkward to say, "I'm the boss, and I say shut up and get on with it." But you can remind subordinates of the situation in other ways. Here, for instance, a senior manager answers a critique sent by a subordinate who disagreed with a new policy:

> You've summed up your case again with force and precision. We've had a lively debate. I, for one, have learned a lot from it. Always being open to argument is one part of my job. Another part of my job is implementing policy decisions. From here on in I know I can count on you to put the same spirit into making this policy work as you put into discussing it . . .

Underlining for Emphasis

<u>Underlining</u> is a way for nudging readers to <u>pay attention</u> to points they might otherwise overlook—or to help the skimming reader to <u>hit the high spots</u>.

When you underline, or use some other form of emphasis (like color shading), <u>make sure you underline all the key words</u>. Your emphasis is an invitation to read the emphasized material more carefully than the other stuff, so vital points that appear without emphasis may get lost.

<u>Limit underlining to important points</u>. When you underline too much or underline details of lesser importance, you mislead the reader and lose the impact of the emphasis.

Getting a Bang from Slang

A divisional vice-president has been confronted with an unwelcome proposal from corporate, suggesting acceptance of a plan put forward by another division. In his response, the VP summarizes the plan, ending with:

> . . . for these reasons Finance recommends that 100 percent of maintenance costs incurred by both divisions be charged to just one division.

Before proceeding with a detailed, dispassionate refutation, the VP writes a three-word paragraph:

<u>Are they kidding</u>?

This slangy interjection gives emphasis and human dimension to what follows. It snaps a picture into the reader's mind. This is not just a recitation of facts. There's a *person* behind it, and that person believes strongly in what he is saying.

Slang, like red pepper, must be used sparingly. But it can be a useful device, to provide a change of pace or to make the abstract concrete.

Sometimes slang can be just what the doctor ordered!

Admit Your Bias

A document arrives on your desk. It's analytical, balanced, and admirably objective in its approach to an issue that is being hotly debated between clearly defined factions in the company. The only trouble with the document is that you know very well that the author has very definite opinions that place him on one particular side of the issue. The words he has written are objective, but as you read you can hear his voice expressing a definite opinion.

So the studied neutrality of the memorandum is nullified. The author may make some good points, but they get lost because the document seems phony in its artificial balance.

Suppose the author had started this way:

My feelings on this subject are well known. I'm on record as being strongly in favor of an aggressive move into the German market at the earliest possible moment. There are logical arguments on the other side. I have done my best to array the arguments, pro and con, fairly, so we can continue to have a productive dialogue.

It's not humanly possible to be 100 percent objective about anything. When you have formed an opinion and expressed it, don't be reluctant to admit your bias when you write about the subject. Your readers will respect you and weigh your arguments more seriously than if you seemed to pretend to neutrality.

The Long and Short of It

You can make a document more inviting by varying the length of the paragraphs.

When you're writing straight narration or exposition, without bullets or tabular material, you may fall into a comfortable rhythm. Your prose jogs along, with sentences and paragraphs of about the same length. This approach gives an orderly, uniform look to the page, but it can induce the reader's attention to wander.

Varied visual patterns on the page refresh the mind and the eye. They provide the small but important changes of pace that keep the reader moving along.

Don't pad paragraphs in order to achieve variety. Cut and compress to make some paragraphs shorter. When two paragraphs are coming out about the same length, see if you can move one or two sentences from one to another. Merge paragraphs that cover similar points.

Visual variety spices a business document.

Hammering Home the Point with Repeated Bullets

When you "bullet" items, it's customary to avoid needless repetition. You don't say:

Applicants are required to

- read the orientation book.
- read the application.
- read the instructions.

It's better to say:

Applicants are required to read the

- orientation book.
- application.
- instructions.

But sometimes you can achieve an interesting effect through repetition in bullets. Here's the conventional approach:

This division is determined to surpass quota in

- volume.
- net performance.
- new accounts.
- return on investment.

But this message is supposed to convey a sense of steadfast dedication. So use repetition:

This SBU is determined to

- surpass quota in volume.
- surpass quota in net performance.
- surpass quota in new accounts.
- surpass quota in return on investment.

Understatement Packs More Punch Than Overstatement

Here's a cry for help:

Two of our four finishing machines are under repair. Our computer is down for at least four days. We are unable to make our regular shipments. Materiel has jammed the warehouse and is piling up in the yard. The forecast is for high wind and torrential rain. We are now ordered to take on an additional emergency run and complete it in half the standard time. The union has called a grievance meeting for next Monday.
   This division is facing a catastrophic situation. Unless we receive urgent assistance at once, we will experience a major disaster.

Well. This telex certainly makes its point. But the sender may come across as panicky; even hysterical. Hysteria does not enhance promotability. The frantic words could leave the lingering impression of unsteadiness in the crunch.

The writer might get better results by understatement. After the litany of difficulties in the first paragraph (which, after all, convey the magnitude of the problem), say:

So you might say we're having a bit of trouble.

The urgency still comes across, but the writer doesn't sound unhinged.

CHAPTER 6

Particular Problems and Special Situations

A lot of your business writing is aimed at the solution of particular problems or at meeting the requirements of special situations. Here's an arsenal of answers, keyed to a number of situations that occur in all kinds of organizations.

Asking for an Extraordinary Effort

Exhortation to do better is usually a waste of time. People are assumed to be doing their best.

However, now and then you may want to ask people to go above and beyond the call of duty. When writing to inspire a maximum effort, acknowledge the extraordinary and limited nature of the request:

We are facing a great challenge. Success in this venture is vital to all of us.

You're all professionals. You've proven your skill and commitment. You always do your best.

On this one I'm asking for more than your best. I'm going to try to reach down inside myself and find resources I didn't know were there. I hope you'll join me. Giving more than your best sounds like a contradiction. You and I know it's not. We know that, when the challenge is great, people can grow bigger to meet it.

That's the kind of challenge we face.

That's the kind of effort we need.

Warning a Subordinate of Poor Performance

People who are turning in subpar performance should be warned that if they don't improve, they will be fired. The warning should be calm, direct, and precise, as a matter of good management. And, these days, it is becoming more important to put such a warning in writing. When the message is on record, the employee can't claim he was not warned. The existence of a written warning can prevent a lawsuit.

Make your warning clear and formal. Don't water it down. However, it's frequently a good idea to accompany such a warning with another message that emphasizes the positive.

A typical warning:

Dear Ted:

As we discussed on May 3, 1991, your job performance has been inadequate in a number of important ways. We talked about these problems and about ways you can improve your performance. We both hope things will work out, and I'll give you whatever help is appropriate. However, you realize that continued failure to perform adequately will lead to your termination.

An accompanying note:

I think we agree that the warning is necessary and justified. With hard work and determination you can bounce back and make the warning unnecessary. I hope so, and I'm confident that you're doing everything possible to straighten out the problems we discussed. I'll be talking with you soon.

Reassuring Someone Who's Made a Mistake

When somebody has blown it, the right kind of note can make a difference in restoring morale and productivity. Put the error in perspective without trying to pretend it's insignificant. Indicate that you know that "to err is human." Mention something positive. Point out, if appropriate, that you yourself have dropped an occasional ball:

Since I know how conscientious you are, I'm sure you feel badly about the Duluth episode. You're usually very much on the ball, so something like this sticks in your mind because it happens so seldom. The important thing is to learn from the experience. That's not always easy. I had a similar problem four years ago . . .

Putting Out the Word That There's Going to Be a Delay

"There will be a slight delay"—in the processing of your order, the boarding of your flight, the mailing of your check. We've all heard the excuses for delay and the promises that it will be "slight." We get cynical about it. We always expect that the wait will be a lot longer than we're told.

Inevitably you have to put out the word that something is delayed—a decision, the completion of an action, the start of a program, a meeting. Inform the readers of the delay. Avoid assurances that the delay will be short, unless you're sure that this is the case. If anything, you may want to prepare your audience for a longer wait than will actually be the case. Let them be pleasantly surprised that the wait is so short, rather than disappointed once again that it's longer than you said.

Avoid explanations unless they are absolutely necessary; they sound like excuses. If possible, suggest something that might be done in the meantime— not make-work, something useful.

> The meeting on streamlining of office procedures, scheduled for September 15, has been postponed. You'll be notified at least a week in advance of the new date, which may not be before the first of the year. This gives us more time to develop scenarios for improvement within our departments.

Floating a Wild Idea

You have an off-the-wall idea. You want to pass it along to the higher-ups. You think it might just have considerable promise. But it may be considered crazy. You don't want to look like a wild-eyed dreamer.

Introduce the idea with a passage that positions it as a serious suggestion but gets you off the hook if it turns out to be totally impractical:

> Here's an idea that might, at first, seem too wild to consider. It seemed that way to me. But as I considered it, I thought it might contain some real possibilities. So I'm willing to risk it and pass the thought along. If you agree that there just might be something here, I'll be happy to work up a more detailed evaluation.

Then present the idea as briefly as possible. Anticipate some of the questions you might be asked—but don't put all the answers into your first memo. Keep it short.

Giving the Truth behind a Rumor

A rumor has been making its way along the grapevine. You've ignored it for a while, but now you want to counter it.

The first requirement in countering a rumor is to have something to replace it with: solid fact. If all you've got is a denial or a vague reassurance, don't put it in writing. Indirect answers to gossip just make the gossip more attractive and credible.

Don't respond to a rumor in writing unless you're sure the rumor is widespread. Otherwise, you're spreading the gossip that you want to stop.

Having decided that you want to write something to short-circuit the grapevine, it's best not to make too big a deal of it. Rather than making your response the subject of a special communication, tack it on to a memo covering a topic allied to the subject matter of the rumor:

> In this connection, I've heard some talk about the possibility that the Seattle operation will be closed. If any of you have heard that one, let me clear it up. Seattle is staying open . . .

Announcing the Resignation of a Key Player

The psychological concept of "cognitive dissonance" states that the mind, confronted with a change in the external situation, revises its beliefs to conform to the new realities. You wanted to buy a BMW. You couldn't afford it, so you settled for a Honda Civic. Without conscious thought, your mind twists itself into a new configuration, in which the BMW's faults are magnified until it becomes practically a piece of junk.

We can see the principle at work sometimes when a key individual resigns from an organization. There is a tendency (as exemplified by the written announcement of the resignation) to minimize the guy's importance and trash his ability. Some of this is deliberate; some is unconscious.

When telling people about the unexpected loss of a key player, don't fall victim to the temptation to knock the departing figure, even indirectly. This diminishes your credibility. And it makes people wonder what you really think of *their* work and *their* importance.

Be realistic:

> Debbi Wheeler has resigned to take a job with Stormes & Sons. Debbi has made significant contributions to our organization. We will miss her.

Leave it at that. Don't tack on inspirational words about how the company will be even bigger and better in spite of Debbi's departure. Just announce the fact.

Announcing a Firing

Some of the most hypocritical and preposterous language in business writing can be seen when the staff is informed that someone has been fired.

Not that the word "fired" is likely to be used. A typical memo might go something like this:

> I'm sorry to have to announce that we will be losing the valuable services of our capable and energetic VP of Procurement Services, Frank Scheisskopf. Frank, whose dedication and ability have meant so much in putting the company where it is today, has decided to return to his first love, independent consulting. I know you share with me a sense of tremendous regret that we are losing Frank. We all wish him well and we are certain that he will be a great success in his new venture. . . .

Of course everybody knows that Frank has gotten the boot, that he leaves kicking and screaming, and that the "first love" he is returning to is the unemployment line.

Firings are inevitable. But the announcement of the firing need not shoot the reader's blood sugar into the red zone. Make the announcement dignified and terse:

> Frank Scheisskopf is leaving us. Frank served this company with energy and dedication, and we wish him well.

Asking for Money—Emphasize the Risk

When requesting larger budgets, line managers tend to build up the advantages and minimize the risks. Financial officers are used to such distortions. They've seen all kinds of pitches for additional funding. Those pitches promise big returns. They rarely dwell on the possibilities of losing money.

So you may be able to make an effective appeal for funding by playing against this trend. Emphasize the risks right at the beginning. Don't minimize them; face them squarely. Finance will find your frankness refreshing. And, besides, you will be doing business with prudent regard to the downside:

> This is a request for $55M supplementary to build two contiguous additions to the Millsburg plant.
> Let me stress right at the start that this is not a risk-free proposition.
> Nevertheless, I think the investment is justified. Let me start with an examination of the principal risks . . .

Nudging a Forgetful Boss

You asked your boss for some action, and you were assured that something would be done. Nothing happened. Now you want to nudge the boss, but you want to do it diplomatically. You don't want to simply repeat your request;

there's an air of nagging futility about that. Nudged into remembrance, the boss may respond, but it may leave a bad taste.

Come up with a reason—or at least a pretext—for sending a reminder:

> Re my request for authorization of extended credit on Empirical Construction—I just got some additional information which should interest you. For me it confirms the urgency of moving fast on this matter. Here are the new facts . . .

The "new facts" need not be a big deal. In fact, the reader may see through them and spot the memo for what it is, a tactful nudge. That's all right. You have not been pushy. You've made your reminder diplomatic. And you've made it likely that you'll get an answer soon, unless there is some other factor besides forgetfulness that is at work here.

Telling Somebody to "Lighten Up"

Occasionally people go overboard, blow things out of proportion, make too big a deal about things. When a subordinate overreacts orally you can straighten things out by talking. When a subordinate overreacts in print, people outside your operation may see the document and get the wrong idea.

Let's say one of your assistants hits you with an apocalyptic message warning that something is radically wrong and that disaster looms. Your own bosses are likely to see copies. You don't want to simply tell the assistant he's all wrong, or greatly exaggerating the situation. That makes him look and feel bad. You need to write a response that straightens out the subordinate without embarrassing him. At the same time you want to reassure the top brass and others that the sky is not falling.

Get out a quick, brief response, with appropriate FYI copies. Give the alarmist good marks for conscientiousness. Indicate that you know things (unknown to him) that make the situation far less serious. Then say that you're handling it.

> Thanks for your report on the situation at InterStation 6. It's always good to be alert and to at least consider the worst possible case, rather than to ignore potential problems. For some time I've been working with Anderson and Chavez on the InterStation 6 problem, and I'm happy to be able to tell you that, while certain superficial aspects may look alarming, the real situation is under control, has been for some time, and is improving . . .

Take bad news seriously enough to make a serious response, even when there's nothing to it.

Announcing a Decision: Talking to the Winners and Losers

When you write a document announcing a decision that has a major effect on various people, you may want to go beyond the bare announcement to offer some muted congratulations to the winners and consolation to the losers:

This decision will be seen, with considerable justification, as a vote of confidence in National Sales Division. However, it is also a vote of confidence in Central Division. If our organization did not have people with maturity and objectivity in all divisions, we would not function as well . . .

Avoid implying any promises to the loser (''Next time Central might come out on top''). Don't agonize about what a tough decision it was to make; few people are interested in the agonies of the decision maker. Make your call loud and clear, and then show you understand the reaction and have confidence in the ability of all concerned to handle it.

Changing Your Mind

You went on record with a forecast, opinion, or decision. But now you've changed your mind. What's the best way to tell people about it?

Start by being precise:

In a memo of 11/13 I informed you that the Incus line would be produced 100 percent at Michigan City.
I have reconsidered that decision. Incus will be produced 50 percent at Michigan City and 50 percent at Baton Rouge.

Then acknowledge the effect:

This change works a hardship on both plants. Michigan City has geared up . . .

Then explain:

You are entitled to know the reason for this change. Here are the new factors that came to light . . .

It's not necessary to apologize. But it is important to give people a chance to ventilate their feelings:

The decision is now final. I know you will cooperate in carrying it out. I'm sure you'll want to discuss this, and I look forward to hearing from you . . .

Assigning Risk Where It Belongs

You receive a proposal that looks good. The originator of the proposal is enthusiastic—so enthusiastic that he presents all the possibilities in glowing terms, while omitting references to risks.

Your gut feeling tells you the risks are there. You don't want to abort the proposal. You have delegated authority and responsibility to the person making the proposal, so you don't want to get too involved in the decision.

Respond favorably—but *indicate that you know there may be more potential problems* than the proposal states. Remind the originator that he carries the responsibility:

> Your idea looks good. I can understand your willingness to take the risks that it entails.

If the originator's glasses are too rose colored, he's likely to look the proposition over again. At least he's on notice that it's his responsibility.

When to Exaggerate the Risk

You should usually spell out the risks in a proposal rather than minimizing them. There are even times when it's to your political advantage to *exaggerate* the risks.

Let's say you're reasonably sure your proposal will be adopted. The idea, in your opinion, will work. You've assessed the risks, and they are minor.

If you present the plan as a sure thing, you won't get full credit when it works. People will yawn and say, "So what?" If it's useful to you to enhance your reputation as a risk taker, build up the dangers somewhat when you make the proposal. You don't have to lie. One good way to build up the perception of risk is by devoting considerable space to it. List *all* the risks, even the minor ones.

There's another advantage to running through all the risks in a proposition. As you're doing it, think about them once again. Something you thought was a minor risk may turn out to be a major one. One of your addressees may have some information or insight on a "minor" risk that warrants reexamination.

By thoroughly covering all potential dangers, you give yourself full credit as a risk manager, and you increase your chances of spotting potentially damaging snags.

Labeling the Risk in a Proposal

Sometimes when we make proposals, there's a tendency to minimize the risk. We may have this tendency because we want to sell the proposition. Or we may have it because we have already considered the risk and discounted it.

When you propose a course of action in writing, include at least one section that spells out the risk, clearly and objectively. This procedure is not only good business; it's good politics. When something goes wrong, there's always a hunt for a scapegoat. You're probably willing to take the heat, but you'll take a lot more heat if you appear to have misled others about the extent of the danger involved.

Some proposal writers weave in continual warnings and qualifiers:

While we have researched this to the extent possible, there is always the chance . . .

Obviously we can't predict with complete accuracy . . .

There are no guarantees . . .

It's better to make a positive, upbeat pitch—and then present the risks in a single section. Label the section appropriately:

Risks—In our judgement, these are the principal risks in the proposed strategy:

- The product line could meet higher than expected resistance at the high end.
- North Jersey might suffer a severe economic downturn.
- One of our main competitors could introduce new and attractive products.

Here is our assessment of the likelihood of these contingencies . . .

Following Up Telephone Conversations: Firm Up the Soft Spots

Telephone conversations can be vague. One party remembers it one way; the other party remembers it another way. Naturally we tend to remember it in a way that is most favorable to our interests.

That's why it's important to follow up significant phone calls in writing.

But how can you remember the exact words that were said on the phone? If the conversation was not taped, there may be misunderstandings.

In your written follow-up, don't try to do the impossible. Put down what was said to the best of your recollection. If you're not sure about a key point, put it down as best you remember it. *If there's a doubt, give yourself the benefit:*

As I recall it, you agreed to pick up 80 percent of the chargebacks on the recall.

In a case where the other party was unclear or perhaps deliberately vague, *put your own meaning on the words:*

You remarked that you feel your department is "probably responsible for most of the chargebacks." I take that to mean that you will pick up the lion's share of the chargebacks: 80 percent was what I suggested, and I assume that's okay with you.

Tell FYI Addressees What's in It for Them

If you're like most of us, a lot of FYI material sluices through your in-box. The trouble is that not all of this material is relevant or helpful—or, if it is, you really have to waste a lot of time getting to the part that interests you.

When you've listed FYI addressees on a long document, help these information addressees out. At the beginning of the document provide a brief rundown of what it contains:

This is a progress report on Project Affinity, covering the period 2/11–2/25. Appendix A lists new accounts opened during the period. Appendix B covers advertising test results. Appendix C includes the most recent changes in the project . . .

Your principal addressee knows this format already; it was followed by previous reports. But the FYI recipients don't know the format. Tell them what's in the document so they can turn to the parts that interest them.

Progress Reports—The Element of Reassurance

A senior manager has asked for a progress report on a project. Here's how the junior manager replies:

In response to your request I have compiled a detailed description of the steps that have been taken so far, along with the schedule for the upcoming quarter. In the appended tables you will find financial projections and copies of intradivision correspondence covering relevant areas of the project . . .

The progress report comes to eighteen pages. It is detailed, painstaking— *and not at all what the senior manager wanted.*

What the senior manager wanted was *reassurance* that the junior manager knows what he's doing, is on track, and will not cause the senior manager to encounter unwelcome surprises.

Put reassurance (when it is warranted) into progress reports:

In brief I am able to report:

1. The project is on track.
2. While we anticipate some challenges ahead, we expect nothing that can't be handled.

3. We are monitoring progress closely. We are in a position to spot problems in advance.
4. You will be kept advised of any such problems.

Now for a brief rundown of the details . . .

Confidential Communications—Avoid Contamination

As a rule, it's safest to assume that any message may be read by persons who are unauthorized to read it. If what you are writing is too hot to be subjected to that risk, then don't write it.

However, there is a whole class of sensitive subject matter that can be called "confidential." It's sent to a restricted number of addressees—say one or two—and readers are enjoined to keep the lid on.

When you transmit confidential material, don't "contaminate" the message with nonconfidential material. For example, a manager writes a confidential memo presenting revised specifications for a product that is still being developed. Then he adds another thought:

> While these changes won't make a big difference in the makeup of your production lines and bench-assembly groups, there will be some room for modification. Group leaders will have to be briefed on how to make the handoffs . . .

The memo goes on to comment on matters that are little more than housekeeping details, not in the same class with the confidential material. This material adulterates the confidential nature of the memo. It reduces the urgency of keeping it secret. It adds to the likelihood that the message will be seen by people who are not authorized at present to see the new specs.

"Give Me Something in Writing"

You've been talking to your boss, pushing hard for a decision that he's reluctant to make. Finally you run up against his next appointment. "I know we need to move on this," he says, "but I have to think about it some more. Give me something in writing, will you?"

What should you put in writing? And at what length? To a great extent the answers to these questions depend on the boss. Does he like a lot of detail, or is he impatient with lengthy documents? Does he expect you to act like an advocate or a recording secretary?

Unless there is a clear reason to do otherwise, your best bet is to write a concise memo that states the question and then *sums up the strongest arguments on your side.* Leave out trivial arguments. Don't repeat assertions that the boss doubted or strongly refuted. Give a reprise of your most compelling points, having first said what you're doing:

Here are the most important reasons for taking this step:

You may think of new points that are worth making. If so, label them:

Since we talked I've pulled out some additional figures on . . .

When you've repeated your arguments, "ask for the order":

May I have your go-ahead on this?

Getting the Correspondence Back on Track

You've written to a colleague in the company (not one of your subordinates) requesting some information or action. You get back an answer that dances around the edges of your request but does not respond. You can't just say, "Hey, this is not what I asked for. Let's get on the ball!" That would not be tactful.

What do you do?

One useful approach is to treat the answer as an interesting message in its own right—but *not* a response to your request:

You raised some useful questions in your letter of 11/16. Your comments will provide helpful background for me when I receive your answer to my letter of 11/5, in which I asked for . . .

You have acknowledged a peripheral contribution—and renewed your request.

When You're Asked for an Opinion

You're asked your opinion of a proposed deal or course of action. As a rule, here's the way your answer should be structured:

What's it about?
What do I think?
Why do I think it?
What leads me to this conclusion?

The following is a model "opinion" memo:

RE: Cormorant Limited proposal

We have been asked to provide a $125M development loan to Cormorant for construction of an industrial park and related shopping mall in Montclair, New Jersey.

I recommend we turn down this request for the following reasons:

1. The North Jersey market is soft.
2. Repayment of the loan would take ten years.

3. There is no assurance that Cormorant can arrange construction funding.
   To assess the current situation in the area, I spoke with . . .
[The memo continues with a distillation of the research conducted by the writer. It winds up:]
   In summary, the project is interesting because of Cormorant's track record, but the source and timing of our repayment are very risky.

Give the Other Side of the Argument

You're involved in a debate within the company on two conflicting plans. You're convinced that plan A is right and plan B is wrong. Naturally you write to advocate your position.

When composing a document to advance your opinion, you're justified in putting your case as strongly as possible. However, it's a good idea to acknowledge the strongest points in the arguments advanced by the other side.

Here's one way to do so: sum up the advantages of your approach. Then sum up, as objectively as possible, the advantages of the other approach. And reiterate your conclusion:

There are pluses and minuses on both sides. On balance, however, I think there are far more pluses on the side of plan A.

By injecting balance into your advocacy, you

- add to your credibility.
- reduce the personal resentment of your opponents.
- display the strength of your arguments in the context of the opposition.

Defusing the Extremes of Controversy

You're putting a very hot topic on the table. There are strong feelings on both sides. In your written announcement of the discussion, you can reduce the heat and save time by stating the extreme positions up front:

This is a controversial topic. At one extreme, some will demand that the entire project be junked—now. At the other extreme there will be a demand that all available development resources be concentrated in this one area.
   I hope we can work together to find a positive solution somewhere between the extremes.

When the thing is treated this way, those who feel most violently are put on notice that they may be stamping themselves as ''extremists'' if they hold forth at great length on their positions. They're not likely to abandon their opinions, but they may be more moderate in stating them, and quicker to engage in the cooperative search for consensus.

Saying No Gracefully

Turndown letters are never pleasant. When you write one, your first task is to be clear that it *is* a turndown. Sometimes people add so much sugarcoating that the message is not clear:

> You have a great many qualifications for the position, and we are unanimous in feeling that you would handle it well. When there are several well-qualified people, the decision rests on other factors, such as amount of time with the firm and availability.
>
> While consideration of all the factors has, in this case, led us to lean toward somebody else, you can be sure . . .

This is supposed to be saying no—a nice "no," but *no*. The trouble is that the recipient, reading it in the most optimistic light, can take it as a "maybe" or even a "wait a while." When the truth hits home, the disappointment (and maybe resentment) will be all the greater.

Be up front about the decision:

> After deliberating long and hard, we have decided to select somebody else for the job of senior administrator.
>
> Your strong qualifications made us consider you very seriously; however . . .

Ways to Say "You're Wrong"

Nobody likes to be caught in a mistake. No matter how well-meaning the correction, it can cause resentment. So when you're pointing out an error, you get the best results when you use the most effective diplomacy.

However, don't be so diplomatic that the point is lost. Be definite in calling attention to the error, but do it in a way that keeps the situation cool.

Spotlight the mistake without assigning it. Don't say:

> You're wrong about the last quarter projections.

The "you" waves a red flag. Instead, say:

> The last quarter projections are erroneous.

You can soften it further by sticking in a pro forma qualifier:

> These last quarter projections are off the mark, I think.

Yet another way to do it is to toss the ball back into the other guy's court:

I have a feeling these last quarter projections don't represent what you'd really like to say. Would you check them out and get back to me?

This last approach permits the inference that the error was a superficial lapse. And it enables the other party to make the correction, rather than having to swallow it.

"Thank You"—Two Magic Words

The thank you note is a useful lubricant injected into the gears of human relations. Some people just forget to send messages of gratitude. Others think such notes are corny. Still others feel that expressions of sentiment have no place in modern management.

Send thank you notes when there's something to be grateful for. Err on the side of sending too many rather than too few. They don't have to be formal memos. Stick a hand-written note onto an official message:

Jerri:

Just a word to say how much I appreciate all you're doing to help us ride out this current difficulty. . . .

A more permanent—and further-reaching—message can be sent when the addressee's contribution is substantial. Make it a more formal memo, with copies to appropriate people. Spell out the contribution.

Saying "thank you" never hurts. Letting others know you've said thank you is good for the thankee—and good for you as well.

Saying Thank You—Specify What It's For

Here's a brief note from an executive vice-president to a division head:

Dear Bill:

This is to say "thank you" for all the help you provided in our recent campaign. I'm very grateful.

The writer has sent a copy to the company's president. This is great—as far as it goes. The trouble is, it doesn't go far enough. The president, not familiar with the details, doesn't know what Bill has done to merit the thanks.

Bill may have worked night and day, making the critical contributions. Or he may have contributed only marginal assistance.

When your written note of thanks is intended (at least in part) to let others know that the addressee has done something that is especially good, specify:

Dear Bill:

Thank you for the important help you provided during our recent campaign. Your day-by-day analyses of competitive reactions, along with your accomplishment in completing your assignment ahead of schedule, were vital to our success. . . .

Going Outside the Organization

The Question of Visibility

You're writing to somebody in another company—a customer, supplier, client, contractor. Obviously you will write the best document you can, using (let us hope) the recommendations you find in this book.

There are certain differences between writing inside and writing outside. For most outside documents the political dimension is reduced in importance. You're less interested in making a favorable impression on most outsiders to whom you write. You just want to get them to do something.

However, industry visibility is an important consideration. Whenever you're writing to people whose opinion might be important, you should give some thought to the self-presentation aspects of the document as well as the overt content. To the extent that you know anything about the addressee, crank in that knowledge. To the extent that you're familiar with the culture of the other organization, reflect it.

Someone May Be Watching

A production executive writes to a supplier:

Your performance has been lousy. Unless it improves we will no longer do business with you. I demand that you

- guarantee quality and delivery on your next order.
- give us a further 10 percent discount as partial compensation for our time and expense in covering your lack of performance.

To the CEO of his own company the production executive writes:

We have been having some trouble with Cornwallis Castings. I've been discussing this with them, and there's every reason to expect that the problems will be straightened out.

Strikingly contrasting tones. The reason is that the production executive is sensitive to the personality of the CEO and the culture of his company—low-key, tolerant, and cooperative rather than confrontational. There's also the fact that Cornwallis Castings is a long-standing supplier, and its top people are friendly with the CEO.

The production executive knows about this relationship, so he pulls his punches in the internal memo. But he lets it all hang out in writing to the supplier—partly because he has to blow off steam somewhere, and partly because he thinks he can get better results this way.

Getting tough in writing is a legitimate technique. It's a two-edged sword, though—a weapon to be used with great care. In this case the writer didn't think his CEO would see a copy of the letter to the supplier. He didn't distribute copies within the company, but the CEO got a copy anyway. He was not happy. He didn't tell the production executive to change his style—he didn't say anything, directly—but he began to wonder if the guy really fitted into the organization for the long term.

When you're writing outside your organization, *always assume it will be read inside the organization*. This caveat doesn't mean you should make drastic changes. It does mean that you may want to apply some commonsense considerations.

Assessing the Dimensions of a Crisis

When you're dealing with an emergency there's no time for the ordinary niceties. Your crisis communications should be blunt and urgent.

Let's say you're dealing at long distance with a major problem in a remote location. Obviously you do as much as you can on the phone. Sometimes you communicate electronically. Here's a typical transmission:

Re your proposed solution:

> Do we have the resources?
> What will it cost?
> How long will it take?
> What happens if it doesn't work?

Respond immediately.

Terse questions. A brusque order. No "please respond," no conventional sugarcoating, no cordial preamble: "Your solution sounds good." No reassurances: "I'm sure you're doing your best to get the facts . . ."

Set a no-frills tone when coping with an emergency. In your style, as well as your words, hammer home the idea that there's no time for fooling around.

Reminding People of Your Credentials

There's a job opportunity opening up within your firm. Ordinarily you would not be considered for it; however, you feel you have certain qualifications that would enable you to do the job well.

You should not be reticent about asking for the job—when the time comes. If you know the position is likely to be created, you can begin to put forward your qualifications early.

Here's how one potential applicant gets in some personal reinforcement in a letter about doing business in the Orient:

We are now learning ways to deal with the unfamiliar business cultures of Japan, Taiwan, and Korea. Looking ahead, I see one potential danger. If and when we move into Eastern Europe, we should not make the mistake of extending these lessons to our methods of operation in that area. My experience with Polish and Czech decision making has convinced me that the situation there will be quite different. . . .

Don't drag it in. But when it's appropriate you may want to make comments that draw upon your experience or qualifications.

Here's What This Is About (but Not in So Many Words)

You're responding to a request made by your boss during a meeting—''Give me a rundown on performance of the new line in large cities as against suburban and rural areas.''

You know the boss likes memos to be crisp and to the point; no wasted words. So you get the information and plunge right in:

Here are the sales figures for the T-650 line for the period 3/6 through 7/2, broken down for metropolitan areas of one million or more, and for stores in suburban towns and rural areas.

The boss looks at this and asks, ''What the hell am I supposed to do about it?'' He's forgotten that he asked for it.

It's best to preface a document with an indication of why you've written it. Even if the recipient knows exactly why it has been written, a copy may be routed to somebody who hasn't got a clue.

You don't have to open with a plodding recitation of the reason for the memo. Jog the recipient's memory indirectly:

After you suggested a rundown of city/town performance on T-650, I got the figures for the period . . .

It's a reminder that doesn't call attention to itself as a reminder.

Saying What Nobody Wants to Hear

Nobody welcomes the messenger with the bad news. The Trojans sneered at Cassandra when she told them the Greeks were hidden inside the wooden horse.

In 1986, General Motors had lost considerable market share. Some key executives saw this decline as just a little glitch. They felt that, with a certain amount of effort, GM would climb back to its accustomed 45 percent.

GM treasurer Leon Krain was obliged to dash these high hopes. Here's what he wrote (as quoted in *Rude Awakening,* by Maryann Keller, William Morrow, 1989):

> Essentially we believe that it is more prudent for the Corporation to capacitize for a 35% North American passenger car penetration level in the 1990s than to invest the capital and engineering resources necessary to achieve 45% penetration.

It's an understated way of saying, "The glory days are gone." Mr. Krain makes his point without rubbing salt in the wounds. The key is his avoidance of terms like "settle for" or "acknowledge that." He states his opinion objectively, without nuance or comment.

When writing bad news, it's a good idea to do a first draft and look it over carefully, asking, "Who's going to be scared, angered, or hurt by this?" Make your point, but take out language that causes needless pain.

"Background Material" . . . ZZZZZZZZZ . . .

People tend not to read the prefaces to books. And they tend not to read sections headed "Current Situation" or "Background" in business documents. They think these sections contain dull collections of things they already know.

All too often, they're right.

Many traditional approaches to formal documents call for a "Status Report" or "Background" section, which usually follows the statement of the topic and comes before the part where the writer gives answers or recommendations.

Let's try to stamp out the background section. Apply the "of course" test. Some of the material can go because everybody knows it. Take what's left and weave it into other parts of your memo.

For example, a typical summary section:

> Our Small Appliance Division has been losing money for four years. Competition from the Pacific rim is increasing. Our domestic competitors are outsourcing

> extensively. The prestige of our lines is eroding. The declining prestige of Small Appliances has been determined by Research to affect sales of other products. . . .

The writer kills this section. The first sentence is reworked to go in the introduction:

> This report explores options for the Small Appliance Division, which has been losing money for four years.

The next two sentences are deemed to be so familiar as to be unnecessary. The remaining two sentences are incorporated into the recommendations section:

> By discontinuing Small Appliances we will strengthen our competitive positions in Home Appliances, Implements, and other divisions. These divisions have suffered because of the "halo effect" from the eroding prestige of the corporate name that has been caused by the decline of Small Appliances. . . .

Fill in the Blanks When You Send a Reminder

A message arrives at your office:

> Remember we'll be talking about high-end penetration when we meet next week.

You're away from the office. The person sitting in for your assistant doesn't know anything about the meeting referred to. So when you phone in to say that you're changing your plans for next week and that you intend to fly to the East Coast, your commitment to this meeting gets lost in the shuffle.

The "reminder" failed to remind because it didn't contain enough information. When you send reminders, always assume the audience needs to be reminded of all the basic details. Thus the message should have read:

> Remember the meeting of the New Business Task Force in the HQ conference room Wednesday, June 23, 2 P.M. We'll be talking about high-end penetration.

Transition: When to Leave Out Links

Some writers worry so much about transition that they overdo it. Every paragraph starts with a laborious effort to connect it with the previous paragraph:

> In the light of these facts . . .
> Having noted those developments . . .
> Now we will consider . . .
> So far this report has covered . . .

These phrases get boring. And they're unnecessary. If your document is organized logically you don't need to go to special lengths to hook it up or tie it in. In fact, if you think you need to use introductory phrases to make a transition clear, it's time to reexamine the structure.

Leave out the links. The train should stay together even when the couplings are invisible.

Progress Report—Pointing Out the Exceptions

There is a tendency to skim progress reports when there is no reason to think that they contain any surprises (which is a good reason to question the practicality of continuing to write progress reports that are not read).

If there is something unusual in the progress report you're turning out, call attention to it right up front:

On the whole the campaign is going as planned. However, in Section 5 you'll find a description of how we have changed the procedure in some significant ways.

Sometimes, when things are not going well, a manager may be tempted to bury the setback in a progress report, hoping it will be missed. That's a big mistake. The culprit will take far more heat when the truth comes out.

The best approach is to alert the reader to the setback right away:

Our reject rate is running higher than it should on two lines. The details are covered in the section on production. A separate memo details the steps we're taking to correct the problems.

Follow-up Notes—Have a Reason for Writing

In a perfect world there would be no reason for follow-up letters, memos, and notes. People would need no reminders. They would pay what they have to pay and do what they have to do the first time.

In the real world it's often necessary to send along reminders. Such follow-ups are more effective when they contain information along with the plea or the prod. The writer doesn't seem to be pushing; the recipient has less reason to resent being pushed.

Here's an example of the ''additional information'' follow-up:

As you put the finishing touches on your report, you may be interested in some interesting numbers I just came across.
[The "new" information follows.]
We look forward to getting your report by next Friday, September 10.

The additional facts need not be earthshaking, but they must be relevant.

What Was Said—and How It Was Said: Contact Reports

Contact reports (or call reports) record what took place during a meeting or conversation with somebody outside the firm (usually a client or prospect). The purpose of this document is to tell about the relevant things that happened during the contact.

Most contact reports simply report the topics discussed and the conclusions reached. However, it's possible to accomplish more. After all, this is a story being told by someone who was present at the contact for the information of someone who wasn't there.

Try giving contact reports greater usefulness by

- including actual quotes.
- reflecting the relative intensity of how things were said.

For instance, a contact report says:

Mr. Evans discussed the possibility of adding a paint department.

The writer could convey more of the actual flavor with a quote:

Mr. Evans said, "If things keep on the way they're going, we may have to put in a paint department."

It's not always possible to relate good quotes verbatim. But you can convey the sense and intensity of what was said:

There was general agreement that they might have to add a paint department. Nobody was enthusiastic.

Making a Summary

There are two ways to summarize. One is simply to *distill*—try to reduce each part of the original to its essentials, *without imposing judgment* on the material. The other method of summarization is to *express an opinion*, conveying in capsule form not just the words of the original, but also the meaning.

A Subjective Summary

A subjective summary does two jobs. It reduces a piece of writing to a shorter length, and it imposes on the summary the opinions of the summarizer.

Here, for example, is a paragraph:

The company's senior management team has been relatively stable for fifteen years. While the firm has shown good results (as measured by market share and return on investment) during periods in which the economy in general and the industry have been healthy, performance fell off during the recent downturn in the industry. While performance of firms throughout the industry was affected, this particular company suffered to a relatively greater degree.

A subjective summary:

The company's senior management team, basically unchanged for fifteen years, was unable to prevent worse-than-industry-average performance during the recent downturn.

When you send out a subjective summary, label it:

I've summarized this document according to my own reactions to the material.

An Objective Summary

When you make a nonjudgmental summary, make sure to retain the balance of the original in terms of the relative length of its parts. If there are two sections of equal length, boil them both down to, say, 20 percent of the original length. If your summary makes one section twice as long as the other, it looks more important.

Summarize with phrases or even single words. You don't have to stick to words used in the original. Use words that get the job done.

An objective summary of this section up to this point:

Making a summary: two methods

    Objective—distill without imposing judgment
    Subjective—express opinion

Retain relative length of original sections
Use phrases or single words

One Sentence per Paragraph

You can summarize a document by boiling down each paragraph to a theme sentence. If the paragraphs are well crafted, the first sentences of the paragraph should state—or at least suggest—the theme, with the rest of the paragraph supporting and developing the theme.

Here's a paragraph:

Staff people should not only be proficient in their disciplines; they should understand their principal role, that of consultant to line managers. This role carries with it the obligation to analyze problems, make recommendations, and communicate those recommendations clearly. It also involves willingness to accept the line manager's decision on whether to accept advice.

Here's a one-sentence summary:

Besides mastery of their disciplines, staff people should be able to serve as consultants to line managers while acknowledging the line manager's final responsibility for the decision.

When Passing On a Document, Provide Guidance

A manager receives a copy of a long document from his boss. Attached is a brief note:

I found this interesting and applicable. I think you will, too.

The document is six pages, covering a variety of topics. The subordinate puts a lot of time and nervous energy into reading it over and over, trying to figure out what the boss means. Is the whole thing applicable? If it's just parts, which parts?

When passing on material, provide guidance. Answer these questions:

Why is it worth reading?
What is the particular relevance?
Which sections are most interesting?
How important is it?

A useful covering note might say:

Note section 3. It describes some interesting alternatives to our hands-on distributor strategy. We're on the right track, I'm sure, but it's worth knowing what other people are doing.

Asking for a Personal Interview

A letter of application ends this way:

I have covered the basic information here, but you will be interested in hearing about these facts in expanded detail. The best way to do this is through a personal interview. I'll call next week. . . .

Although the writer thinks this is a practically irresistible proposition, the reader (alas!) finds it highly uninviting. The writer assumes an interest that may not exist. Even if the reader is somewhat interested, he or she is likely to be a little resentful of the assumption. ("How the hell does he know I'll be interested?") Also, the promise that the reader can hear about the facts already covered in "expanded detail" lacks allure.

When you're pitching for a personal interview (whether it's with your own CEO or a potential employer), give the reader an answer to these questions:

Why should I spend half an hour with this person?
Will it be helpful, stimulating, or intriguing?
Will I hear anything new?

Sell the new and the interesting. Don't assume that the reader will be interested; that's for the reader to decide:

In a letter, all you can cover is the nuts and bolts. I have some ideas, and perhaps some information, that may interest you. At least I hope I can put forth one or two suggestions that you may not agree with, but that you might find stimulating. Would you talk with me? I'll call next week. . . .

Integrating Technical Data into Nontechnical Documents

A senior executive is reading a memo from a department head recommending a new electronic-mail system. The document flows along, describing the system and its benefits in reasonably clear language, accessible to the non-specialist:

The system is consistent with company-wide message management standards; therefore, no user retraining is necessary.

Then the senior executive hits this passage:

Operating environment on the gateway equipment:

IBM PC, XT, AT, PS/2
512K RAM
20 Mb local hard disk
Commu-App Spec CAS compatible

And so on. The senior executive doesn't understand these specs. The misunderstanding clouds the executive's reaction to the rest of the document. The technical passage fails to answer key questions:

What does this mean?
Why is it important?

Could the technical material be eliminated? The writer of the memo knows that the audience includes technicians as well as line managers. So the specs need to be included.

What's the best way to handle them? The writer wants them in the main body of the memo, rather than in a separate document or in an appendix. Can the specs be translated into language accessible to everybody? No; the effort would be ludicrous.

The best way to integrate such material into the main body of a general document is to label it for what it is:

> The following operating specifications will be of primary interest to technical staff.

An introductory note should inform (even warn) readers of material that is meaningful only to specialists. Such an introduction enables nonspecialist readers to skim over the stuff without feeling they are missing something vital to them.

Saying Something Nice When There's Not Much to Say

One of your people has sent you a long, detailed report that is a thorough disappointment. It misses the point, and it comes to wrong conclusions. Also, it's written clumsily.

The person worked hard on it. That fact doesn't make it good, but it does indicate the person is trying.

How critical should you be in your response?

First, separate form from content. The form is unsatisfactory; so is the content. Handle them separately.

Respond to the sense of the memo. Acknowledge the effort that went into it. You're not going to give A for effort, but maybe a C + would be reasonable. Your response starts:

> Your report of June 16 shows that you've given a lot of thought to the subject. It stimulated me to examine some of these points again. As part of a continuing dialogue let me tell you where I disagree with a number of your central positions.

Note that this runs counter to the conventional approach to criticism, which is that you talk about the activity, not the person. Here, instead of saying "Your positions are wrong," you say, "I disagree with you." (You've also said it "stimulated me," which is not lavish praise, but it's at least something.)

You've dealt with the content in your response. Deal with the *form* face-to-face, perhaps as part of the regular performance review. You may want to use this book in helping the subordinate to write better.

Changing the Subject

You're asked to write a memo responding to a specific question. You think the question is wrong: too narrow, focusing on the wrong thing, whatever. You do not want to reply by quibbling with the question; such an attempt might imply that you don't know the answer.

Repeat the exact question you've been asked; sketch out an answer under the terms of that question; then broaden the field to accommodate the response you really want to make.

> You asked for ideas on a campaign to meet the advertising blitz being mounted by MacIntyre. [MacIntyre is a larger company competing with your company in selling chain saws and power mowers.]
> We could go head-to-head with MacIntyre in magazine and broadcast advertising aimed at the designated target market, relatively affluent suburban homeowners. This campaign would have to find ways to offset the appeal of MacIntyre's new, more powerful engines and restyled casings. But there may be a better approach than head-to-head competition: an end run. MacIntyre's beefed-up commitment to luxury-class lines gives us an opening. We can turn the simplicity and less-powerful motors of our VLU-60 and VLU-90 lines from liabilities into assets by planning a campaign to exploit the broader, more blue-collar market . . .

This memo is not saying, "We don't have a realistic chance of beating the competition in the market where we have been competing." Nor does it say, "We've been following a faulty strategy."

Not saying those things in so many words, that is. The points are made, but they are placed in a nonconfrontational context.

Sometimes you have to change the subject because, if you stay on the subject that has been posed, you're going to make people so mad they can't be objective about your ideas. So switch subjects. Shift to a more favorable ground, but do it in a way that seems to keep you on the old ground.

Realism: Recognizing the Existence of the Grapevine

Every office has two communications networks: the official network and the unofficial one, which flourishes in the lunchrooms, the rest rooms, the copier rooms, the refreshment areas—anyplace where people get together to exchange the latest rumors.

Astute executives know what's being said on the unofficial network. When appropriate, refer to this fact of business life:

The grapevine is saying that a "restructuring" is imminent.

Let's examine that proposition. In one sense, this organization is always going through "restructuring." A company that doesn't continually change and adapt is a company in trouble.

However, let's look more closely at the implication that there may be a substantial change in the organization of the manufacturing divisions . . .

By acknowledging the grapevine you show that you're not isolated in an ivory tower. And your words are read with more attention because they seem more rooted in the real world.

Saying No Gracefully

When you say no—refuse a request, deny a raise or promotion, whatever—be definite enough so that your "no" is read loud and clear. At the same time, make the negative response as pleasant as possible.

Some managers scorn sugarcoating. They ask, "Why be insincere?" Well, first of all, finding something good to say is not necessarily insincere. If there's nothing nice to be said at all, why do you have anything to do with the other party? Second, while sugarcoating may be hypocrisy, it is a conventional way of softening the blow. The other person knows the words don't mean all that much, but if they're written gracefully, they help. At least they show that the writer thinks enough of the relationship to make the effort.

Here's a refusal note that does the job:

I'm sorry to tell you that we have selected another supplier for the Welkin project.

You were among the finalists. Your bid, although it was not within the three lowest, attracted considerable interest because of your track record and your understanding of our needs.

We will keep you informed of future projects, and we hope to be able to do business with you someday.

Key Your Document to Your Most Important Readers

Two department heads have been exchanging written communications for some time about a joint project. They're both up to speed on the project, so they're able to keep their writing short. But suddenly one manager sends a long memo, defining certain frequently used terms and recapping recent actions. The other responds with a similarly detailed document, seemingly much longer than necessary.

What has happened?

What has happened is that a senior manager, previously uninvolved, has asked ''to be kept informed on how things are going.'' She didn't ask to receive a formal briefing or to be sent the file of correspondence. (The file is available anyway, should she want it.)

By sending each other detailed memos, the managers are filling in the necessary gaps in the senior manager's knowledge without making a bigger deal out of it than is warranted.

When you learn that a wider audience (previously unincluded) is starting to look at your correspondence, make the necessary adjustments. Put in the amount of detail needed for the newcomers, even though it is superfluous for those who have been in on it from the beginning.

Handling Complaints

Acknowledge the Importance

Handling complaints by mail is a skill that can be used by anyone in business, not just customer-relations specialists. The same techniques used to mollify irate customers can be used in responding to teed-off contacts inside and outside the organization.

Don't minimize the complaint. Complainers always think their problems are more important than do the persons on the other end. But if you try to tell the guy with a grievance that his beef is insignificant, he will just get madder, even if your case is overwhelming.

So whenever you deal with a complaint, it's best to give the matter the same weight—at least at the outset—as the complainer. If anything, take it *more* seriously:

I take this very seriously. We are doing everything we can to clear the matter up.

Don't Blame the Complainer

Someone has disputed one of your actions. The complainer's facts are wrong. You might feel justified in sending a stinging response:

If you check paragraph 3 you will see that you are in error. We have complied with every aspect of the directive . . .

Handle the response as if, spurred by the gripe, you have looked further into the situation and just discovered the facts that will now clear things up:

Your comments led us to reexamine the directive. A close reading of paragraph 3 seems to indicate that we have, indeed, complied with every aspect of the document. Would you take a fresh look and give me your judgment on this?

Empathize and Sympathize

Identify with the complainer; let the complainer know you understand his problem and feel his distress; manifest willingness to listen:

I know how tough this is for you. You are right to be concerned. Please don't hesitate to tell us about developments as they occur. Meanwhile we are working as hard as we can to solve the problem . . .

Ventilation allows people to blow off steam. You may not be able to do much about the complaint. You may think it's exaggerated, or the other person's fault. Nevertheless, it's a good idea to express sympathy and willingness to listen.

Make Concessions Gracefully

The squeaky wheel gets the grease. Sometimes you have to give in to a complainer, even when the complaint is unjustified or overstated.

Resist the temptation to make your concession meanspirited:

Rather than keep this controversy going, we will agree to the charge-off, even though we don't see any justification for it.

Make the concession gracefully, without being flowery about it:

We will agree to the charge-off. While we still have some questions, you have made your case forcefully and responsibly. Thank you for letting us know about this problem. We're setting up procedures to make sure such a question will not come up again.

This concession agrees without admitting fault. It credits the complainer for cooperation. It refers to a revised procedure. And it sets no precedent that might be costly in the future.

Bringing a New Boss into the Picture

Acquaint a new boss with what you're doing—and what you're thinking. Brief the new top person with a separate short memo for each significant project you're working on. (Separate documents are better than one long document covering everything; the short ones are easier to digest and file, and enable the reader to focus on one topic at a time.)

Each new-boss briefing memo should

- summarize the situation.
- tell what you're doing.
- offer your observations and recommendations.
- specify the steps to be taken next.

CHAPTER 7

Persuasion and Pressure

Getting others to do what you want them to do—this is one of the keystones of success. It's not enough to be smart or to be right. If other people don't buy your ideas or respond to your initiatives, you're doomed to futility.

A lot of managers are practically irresistible in person and highly convincing on the phone, but weak in print. Since modern high-level management requires that the manager's influence be exerted over long distances, persuasive writing is indispensable to many diverse individuals.

Make It Easy to Say Yes

You're writing a "sales talk." You make a case, and you want agreement from the addressee. Not hesitation, not delay, not rebuttal—agreement. Moreover you want that agreement in writing.

Make it easy for the other guy to agree. Direct-mail people know that response goes up dramatically as you make it easier to respond—through a postage-paid "bounceback" card, check-off boxes that make it unnecessary to write much, an 800 number.

Give the addressee an easy way to go on record immediately as saying yes. Avoid open-endedness:

> I look forward to your agreement to this procedure. Please let me know as soon as possible.

This approach invites a reluctant addressee to have second thoughts, think up objections, or come back with a conditional assent:

> In general I agree, although I wonder if you could clarify . . .

Provide a simple, definite means of response:

When you've read this, please initial a copy and send it right back.

Or:

To save time, just transmit "OK #72-633."

Put the brief response together with your original message, and you have the record of assent.

Anticipating Disagreement

You're writing to someone who has already taken a strong position in opposition to the course you're recommending. The previous exchanges have been spirited, even heated. You feel that you have something new to contribute to the dialogue, but you're not naive enough to expect instant conversion—or even a totally open mind.

What you want is a fair hearing. You want the other party to read what you have to say with at least a degree of objectivity.

Try an opening like this:

You're going to disagree violently with some of the conclusions and recommendations in this letter. I hope you will examine my reasons for making them.

"Disagree violently" probably overstates the case. This exaggeration is deliberate. Most people don't want to be seen as unreasonable in their opposition to anything. By acknowledging the disagreement in advance—and exaggerating it a little—you have not won your case, but you've alerted the other party to be ready for some unwelcome words. And you've probably increased your chances of objective consideration.

Start with a Provocative Question

When you're writing to persuade, you can occasionally achieve a striking opening with a provocative question that encapsulates the opposing argument. Here's an example:

Who needs another layer of bureaucracy?
That's a fair question with regard to the proposal for a policy review board. Here is my answer.

This opening goes to the very gut of the opposition. It shows that the writer is familiar with the nature of the opposition and is willing to face it.

And there's a good-natured tolerance expressed by the opening question. It sets the tone for a spirited exchange, without any punches being pulled.

Got a Weak Link? Label It

If you've done a reasonable prewrite workout you have asked yourself, "What's the weakest part of my document? How can it be strengthened?"

Let's be practical. You may discover a weak link in your argument—and you may not be able to strengthen it, at least not without taking too much time.

There are ways to paper over a weakness—but most of them are ethically dubious and probably self-defeating.

Instead of trying to conceal the weak link, think about labeling it for exactly what it is. Here's how it might be done:

> The research underpinning for this part of the plan is not as strong as I would like. I have made inferences from the data available. Maybe you can suggest other ways in which the assumptions can be proved or disproved.

People who ask for help instead of pretending to perfection enhance their stature and get the job done better.

You may want to be even more candid:

> This is a shaky argument. I admit that. Nevertheless, my gut tells me the idea will work.

Your instinct can be extremely valuable. Be willing to express your hunches—but don't mislabel them as fact.

Using Quotations for Authority

A product group manager wants to persuade her marketing vice-president to approve a change in store display policy for certain products in her area. She writes:

> Our fight for shelf space for Jumblies in the snack section takes tremendous effort—effort that may not be paying off. Jumblies tend to get lost in that section, because of the size of the package and because of the hybrid snack/sweet nature of the product.
>
> I recommend that we design a freestanding display that can tie in with current Jumblies media advertising, appeal to impulse buyers, and get the product out of the clutter.

The group manager has done her homework. She has formulated a rule of thumb that she thinks is an apt one. She could put it in this way:

> Packages less than 6″ x 4″ x 3″ are more likely to be selected from a freestanding dump environment than from an ordered row.

The manager wants to get credit for her concept. At the same time she wants favorable reaction on her idea. So she uses authority. The company uses the services of Walter Coyle, formerly director of marketing, now a consultant to the firm. Coyle is highly regarded by most in the company, including the addressee.

So the manager talks over her idea with Coyle, who thinks it may be quite valid, although further study should be made before carving it in stone. Then she writes:

> As Walter Coyle agrees, there is a tendency for packages like Jumblies to work better in a freestanding dump environment than a shelf environment.

She has watered down the statement a little, but she has given herself the great advantage of an authority whose endorsement will help in winning the point.

Leaving the Obvious Unsaid

When you're writing to make a point, it's common sense to spell out that point as clearly as possible. When you've built a chain of solid evidence leading to an obvious conclusion, you wind up by stating that conclusion.

But not always. Occasionally you can achieve a striking effect by building up to the conclusion and then *understating* it—or leaving it to the reader to figure it out.

In the following excerpt, the writer sums up a persuasive case:

> If we do not roll out this product within three months, we will be overtaken by competition.
> In test markets, initial results were mediocre, but the revised advertising campaign produced good test scores over the final five weeks.
> By all but one measurement, consumer response is distinctly favorable. The one negative measurement is the least reliable of those we use.
> If we abort the project now we will pay a high price in dollars, in market share, and in prestige.
> Fail-safe steps protect us through the entire rollout.
> Draw your own conclusions.

Sometimes, at the end of a series of punches, the light jab has a greater effect than the devastating uppercut.

Persuade Words

Putting "You" in the Picture

"You" is a great persuade word. When trying to get somebody to do something, use "you" to help underscore the benefits.

For example, a writer is trying to persuade an engineer to specify certain equipment in a manufacturing process. The writer might say,

> According to the enclosed report, our G-250 wheels last an average of 14 percent longer than conventional wheels in applications similar to those carried on in your operation.

But here's another way to say it:

> The enclosed research shows that the G-250 wheels last 14 percent longer than conventional wheels, on the average. You may do even better in your application. But even if you show only a 10 percent improvement, you'll be able to report significant savings. And you'll be able to devote more time to other important aspects . . .

Help the addressee to see himself or herself enjoying the benefits. "You" helps you to personalize the benefit.

"You Can Be Sure . . ."

A document setting forth some revised policies for sales divisions arrives on the desks of division managers. The managers read it with varying degrees of anxiety. Each is looking first for changes that will limit the authority of divisional managers, alter territorial responsibilities, or have other negative effects.

It happens that there aren't any negative effects in this document. But the division managers don't have that information, so they're not as relaxed and objective as they should be in studying the policy statement.

Anticipate your readers' anxieties. Will your readers be worried about anything that may be contained in your words? Maybe they have reason to be worried. But if they don't, do yourself and your readers a favor by dispelling the anxiety at the outset:

> You can be sure that none of these changes will affect the authority or responsibility of . . .

By clearing up such questions at the start, you allow the reader to focus on the really important elements in the document.

Dramatize the Favorable Outcome

The words used to describe an objective can help people to appreciate what achievement of that objective will mean to them personally.

> The following goals have been designated for this SBU for fiscal 1992:
>
>> 5 percent increase in market share
>> 15 percent increase in gross sales
>> 18 percent increase in net profit
>
> If we devote our best efforts to the task, these objectives, although high, can be met . . .

That's one way to lay out the objectives. Here's another:

> By the close of fiscal 1992 we will be enjoying
>
>> a 5 percent increase in market share.
>> a 15 percent increase in gross sales.
>> an 18 percent increase in net profit.
>
> This will be the situation when—and if—we meet our objectives. If we are successful, we will be proud of what we've done. And we'll be financially rewarded as well . . .

Obviously words on paper are not decisive in achieving goals. But written descriptions of goals should be motivational rather than deadening. Help readers visualize what achievement of the goals will mean to them.

Make Agreement Easy

When you want the addressee to say yes, make agreement easy. One way to do so is by telling the reader to include the ''yes'' in a message that the reader will enjoy writing.

For instance, the manager writing the following document wants a marketing department to submit certain data earlier than has been the case in the past. The data will be incorporated into a compilation that will be of use to all marketing groups.

> You probably want to be on the preferred list to receive these reports before they are distributed generally. Just get in touch with Si Miller to arrange same-day transmission of your results to him. At the same time he'll set up the procedures to give you an advance crack at the reports . . .

"You Can Help" Rather than "I Want"

In making a request of a subordinate, emphasize the cooperation of the other party rather than your own desires:

> To show that marketing staff is fully involved in the campaign, I want you to visit each branch office in October.

That's clear enough. And it has the advantage of giving the reason for the activity. Just issuing a flat order seems abrupt:

> You are directed to visit each branch office in October.

There's a better way:

> You can help to show that marketing is fully involved by visiting each branch office in October.

It's still an order. But it combines an explanation and a persuasive emphasis on the word "you."

Collection Letter—The Threat

When previous collection letters have not worked, you add another element: the *threat*. In 1881 they did it this way:

> Sir:
>
> Feeling much disappointed by your failure to settle my account according to promise, I am compelled to say that the profits of my business will not admit of longer credit. At the same time, I should be sorry to inconvenience you, and will therefore fix the 27th instant for payment; after which it will be quite impossible for me to wait, however unpleasant the alternative.
>
> > I am, sir, yours obediently,

"However unpleasant the alternative!" The threat is not spelled out, but it is very plain. A modern version might go this way:

> You have been asked repeatedly to settle your account, and now I'm afraid we've just about run out of time. We've given you as much leeway as we're allowed to—more, actually. But now, although I regret it, we have to put the collection machinery in motion, unpleasant as that may be. I've been able to get them to wait until June 16 before they start coming down on you; but that's it. Please pay in full before then; it's out of my hands.

Ominous. Refer to a process that is hard-boiled and maybe even brutal. Don't specify. Say you're sorry to have to turn it over to these tough collection experts. Then provide a very brief window of opportunity, giving the other person just enough time to pay up and forestall the harsh retribution that is otherwise inevitable.

Collection Letter—Be Clear, Forceful, and Brief

When you're writing to urge somebody to pay a bill, or to fulfill some other commitment that is clearly understood between you, get right to the point. No wandering down side paths. No sugarcoating. Be calm, but be very clear.

Back in the nineteenth century, before the telephone, most business was done in writing. While the language of that day was more formal and courtly than the language we use today, the principles haven't changed much. You might be interested in this suggested letter, printed in the *National Encyclopedia of Business and Social Forms,* published in 1881:

> Dear Sir:
>
> As I have a heavy payment to meet on the 20th of this month, I must beg you to give immediate attention to my account, which has already run far beyond my usual limit of credit. You have not made any payment on this account for the last three months, and I must really urge greater promptness on your part, as the nature of my business does not allow me to remain out of my capital so long.
>
> Very Respectfully Yours,

The writer underscores the seriousness of the situation, spells out the delinquency, and urges immediate payment, pointing out that he, the writer, is suffering harm. This last element is particularly important. Debtors often find it easy to rationalize delay. ''It won't hurt them to wait another couple of weeks.'' Don't allow any grounds for rationalization. Spell it out that the other guy is delinquent and it *hurts*. In many cases, though assuredly not in all, this can be enough.

A modern version of the ''it hurts'' collection letter might look like this:

> Since I have to settle all my outstanding bills by the end of this month, it is now essential that you pay your account in full. (I enclose another copy.) Your final payment is now more than ninety days overdue. I'm sure we both agree that this is not a good way to do business. Please send full payment right away, as I can't afford to carry your delinquent account any longer.

Ask for the Order

A customer has requested some unusual assistance. The assistance is provided. Having arranged for the help, the marketing manager writes the customer a letter that concludes like this:

We have made every effort to provide you with the assistance you requested. Please don't hesitate to let us know if we can be of any further service in this matter, or in any other way.

We value our association with you, and we are always ready to help. I hope our relationship will continue to prosper.

This is nicely put—perhaps too nicely. After all, the marketing manager's company has made an unusual effort to help this customer. The wording of the letter seems almost to say that the company exists only to be of service.

Nonsense! The company exists to do business at a profit. When you do something for somebody else, don't be coy about asking for something in return. In this case the manager might have written:

You can be of help to me as well. Within the next few days our representative, Pete Aron, will call to set up an appointment. Pete is ready to show you a new product that we think you'll find very interesting.

We look forward to an expanding, mutually helpful, and mutually profitable relationship.

People expect you to ask for the order. And they respect you for it.

Helping Somebody Else Sell for You

Persuasion is tough enough when you're doing it on your own. When you have to do it through a third party, it's a lot tougher.

Let's say you're writing to sell an idea to the president of a company. The only trouble is, you can't write direct to the president. You have to go through channels. The vice-president to whom you're writing can't say yes. You count on him to represent you.

First, assure the person to whom you're writing that you consider him a key player. *Address him as if he were the decision maker* (even though you know he's just the go-between). Make your pitch:

When you weigh this proposal against the others, please remember our track record: TenSiCom has independently verifiable proof of every one of its claims.

Word the pitch in a way that makes it easy for the recipient to use your exact words in passing along your proposition:

I think you'll come to the following conclusions:

TenSiCom's on-site training will help us get into full operation at least two weeks earlier.

Our production staff will react enthusiastically to TenSiCom's ease of operation.

When we call TenSiCom with questions, we'll talk to knowledgeable technicians.

To the extent possible, word your presentation *exactly* as you'd like the reader to pass it along. You're writing a script. The easier your words are to use, the more likely it is that your reader will use them, orally or in writing.

"We"—Persuasion by Joining Forces

"We" is a useful word in persuasion because it says "you're not on your own; you've got company and you've got help; I'm with you on this . . ."

Managers are constantly looking for ways to motivate subordinates. One of the best motivators is the repeated demonstration that the boss is sympathetic, interested, and actively involved. However, professions of higher-level involvement are undermined by memos like the following:

September 1 is the kickoff date for the fall productivity drive. You have been assigned your individual and group goals. You've had the opportunity to discuss the project at departmental meetings. I know you will all exert your best efforts, and I look forward to the greatest success yet . . .

People might get more of a feeling of top-to-bottom effort if they received a message like this:

We kick off our fall productivity drive September 1. We've all got our goals, and I know we're all going all out to achieve them. In our departmental meetings we've had a chance to talk over ways and means of hitting the target. Let's give it our best shot . . .

Convincing the Disbeliever

When you're writing to somebody who is going to be hard to sell, you've got a special challenge.

First, think about the nature of the reader's skepticism. Is the reader on record as opposing what you're proposing? Or a particular part of it? Or do you just have a general idea that the person you're addressing is tough to sell?

If the latter is the case—the addressee is just hard to sell as a matter of course—your best bet is just to do the best job you can. Make sure of your facts. Marshal your arguments cogently. Write with brevity and impact. Package your ideas as best you can, and see what happens.

If the addressee has already expressed an opinion, study that opinion. Think about it; maybe the other guy is right. If you still think you're right, then you have a mark to shoot at. Put together the arguments that you think ought to make the addressee change his or her mind.

Then get right to the point:

> You wrote on May 19 that the proposed on-the-job training program would cost more than results would warrant. This memo is an effort to respond to that judgment . . .

Closing on a Minor Point

Sometimes when you're writing to get agreement, the other person may be convinced by your logic and cowed by your authority—but still find it hard to give in. It's a matter of saving face.

Make it easier for the other party. Provide the opportunity to make a choice on a subordinate aspect of the question. For example, a manager wants the addressee to convene a special meeting, something the other guy is reluctant to do. The writer might put it this way:

> I have considered your objectives carefully and decided that the meeting must take place no later than next Thursday.

Instead, the writer offers a measure of autonomy:

> My preference would be for the meeting to include just you, me, and your three department heads. You would probably prefer to include the section chiefs as well. If you decide to have them, I'll go along—that is, if you can get them all together by next Thursday.

Avoid Loopholes When Giving an Assignment

In writing to instruct a subordinate to complete a task by a specified date, a manager is specific about every aspect of the job. He thinks he's making it clear that the project is important, must be started right away, and must be completed on time.

However, the writer makes the mistake of leaving a loophole:

> Although the specifications for this component are not yet available, they should be available shortly.

When the job is not done on time, the manager asks, ''What happened?'' He is told, ''We were waiting for you to supply the specifications.''

The writer's intent was that the addressee had to get those specs. But this requirement was not spelled out.

Closing all the loopholes is especially important when you're dealing with someone who is less than enthusiastic about doing what you want. Review the document with this question in mind: If I wanted to delay or to claim I was waiting for some other step, could I use anything here as an excuse?

On-the-ball people don't use loopholes as alibis—at least, not usually. But people who are under pressure sometimes look for escape clauses. Don't provide any.

Citing Authority to Support Your Position

Quotation of authorities to support one's position is a standard technique in persuasive writing. It's a good ploy for writers who are trying to make points about politics, social issues, artistic matters, and so on. The writer brings in a powerful reinforcement to help in the job of persuasion.

People in business don't use authority enough. Few business documents contain telling quotations. That's understandable. The use of quotations may seem too literary. Citing an expert can look, to some individuals, like a pointless excursion. Ralph Waldo Emerson said, "I hate quotations. Tell me what you know."

And yet an apt quotation can work well when the authority you cite carries weight with your audience.

As you read the business and general press, note and clip material you think is especially insightful. Keep a file of good quotes. You can use them in speeches. (It is interesting that citations are used much more freely in talks than in written presentations.)

When the right moment comes up, use a pertinent quote to support your position. The quote can't look as if it's artificial or dragged-in. It has to be on the button, relevant, and attributed to an authority who is credible to the reader. When these conditions are met, you can add impact and distinction with a quote:

We need to reexamine our goals and define them in a way that everyone understands. As Peter Drucker says, "Management by objectives works if you know the objectives. Ninety percent of the time you don't."

Adroit quotation supports your point and also shows that you read and retain what you read.

Framing the Document with a Repeated Question

When you want people to take a situation seriously and to devote their best efforts to thinking about it, you can achieve impact by posing a question at the start of the document—and then winding up with the same question:

How much control should Corporate exert over the budget decisions of divisions?

We are in the process of formulating a policy in this area. The policy should be flexible enough to offer wide entrepreneurial latitude to the operating units, and at the same time firm enough to enable Corporate to carry out its mission of effective financial planning.

You will all have a chance to contribute to the forging of this policy. Here are some of the factors to be considered.

[The memo details various factors, then concludes:]

It's a vital question for all of us. How much control should Corporate exert over the budget decisions of divisions?

CHAPTER 8

Cut It Short

Nobody ever complained that a memo or report wasn't long enough. Here's a brief selection of techniques for making your documents shorter.

Shortcuts to Brevity

Apply the "Of Course" Test

Many reports and memos contain material that is familiar to the reader. The writer includes the unnecessary material because he or she was "thinking out loud" when composing the document, or because of a feeling that it's better to put in too much than too little, or through carelessness or fatigue.

When you look over a document, apply the "of course" test to everything in it. If you could reasonably say "of course" before any statement—take it out.

"To Sum Up . . ."

Some documents conclude with a paragraph (which may or may not be designated as a summary) recapping what has gone before:

The total market potential for inorganic coatings is estimated at more than $2 billion annually. More than half of this potential lies in the state bridge market. (See Attachment A.)

Now is the time to launch a national marketing campaign that promotes the new technology. Because the bridge market is specialized and easily identified, IC will use its own sales force to handle the business. The efforts of the sales force will be supported by presence at trade shows and conventions attended by state public works officials.

> With a potential market of more than $1 billion in state bridge work, we should move quickly on a sales campaign to reach decision makers in this area.

The final paragraph can be cut. It sums up what has gone before without adding anything new.

Cut the Body, Keep the Summary

As noted in the previous section, you can eliminate summary windups that add nothing to what has gone before. But, hey, wait a minute—maybe you can *keep the summary* and get rid of all the other stuff:

> To: Russ Camberwell
> From: Andy Haslik
> Subject: Minimum call standards
>
> During my visit to St. Charles the other day, we had a chance to discuss various phases of regional performance. One of the things we touched on was daily calling average. While we both agreed that it's necessary to make as many calls on physicians as possible, you pointed out that a quota that requires too many calls cuts down on planning time and may restrict our reps in their ability to make adequate presentations of the full line, not only to physicians but to their office staffs as well.
>
> Our quota for some time has been an overall average of seven physician calls per day. In the light of our conversation, along with the responses of other regional managers, I have concluded that the quota should be revised downward to five physician calls per day. This revision in quota should be accompanied by a corresponding increase in the time spent in in-depth selling within the office or facility.
>
> As of now, therefore, the call quota is five physicians per day, a change that should make it possible to do more effective selling on each call.

With a little revision and expansion, the windup paragraph could be the whole memo.

> As of now the call quota is revised to five physician calls per day. This change, based on our conversation the other day, along with the reactions of other regional managers, should make it possible to do more effective selling on each call.

Relegate Less Important Stuff to the Back

Everything in a long document may be necessary. But everything may not be equally important. There may be some material that does the necessary but unexciting job of providing the nuts and bolts. When you're writing to more than one addressee, some things that are fresh and important to one reader may be more familiar or less important to another.

You can speed up a document by removing some bread-and-butter material from the main body and placing it in an appendix. Signal the addendum clearly at the appropriate place in the body.

Job descriptions for director of research and associate director of research are covered in Appendix A.

The placing of supplementary material in appendixes makes things easier for readers, who can separate the appendix and place it next to the body copy.

Break Up a Long Document

Brevity lies in the eye of the beholder. Sometimes you can achieve a feeling of brevity by breaking a long document into two or more shorter documents.

At first this suggestion may seem illogical. After all, when you split one memo into two, you're almost certain to use more words because of the repetitions necessitated by the split. Nevertheless, you achieve the impression of brevity.

When we pick up a document, our eyes and brains start fresh. We tend to get the general idea pretty quickly. Then, as we read on, attrition sets in. Attention runs downhill, even when the material is important and well handled.

The material that comes two or more pages deep in a memo must battle this attrition of attention. The reader, without realizing it, is beginning to be bored. The reader—action oriented—is getting impatient to turn to something new.

By breaking a document up you take advantage of your readers' drive to get on with something else. The simple act of picking up a fresh piece of paper sets the boredom indicator back to zero. Even though the second document is tied in with the first, your reader approaches it as if it were new.

Whenever your document is going to run to considerable length, look for ways to break it up. If it's possible to separate the material under two or more headings, consider writing separate documents for each.

You want the whole thing to be read at one sitting, so you attach the documents to each other in the proper order. In the first document run a ''preview'' of the next:

There are some new and important guidelines for evaluating phone reps. Read the memo that follows (Ref 7/12 930).

Cut the First Sentence

When the topic is indicated in the heading, you need not write an opening sentence that serves only to tell what the document is about. (This rule does not apply when you're writing to someone whom you know to be a chronic skipper of headings. Some people are like that.)

> To: Jeff Halvorsen
> From: Ann Moore
> Ref: February retail promotions
>
> This memo concerns our February retail promotions. We plan to focus on three areas . . .

Since the opening sentence just repeats what's in the heading, drop it. Get right to the action: "We plan to focus on three areas . . ." Any reader who is unsure can simply glance at the heading—that's what it's for.

Cutting a superfluous opening sentence does more than just eliminate a few words. It gives the reader a feeling of businesslike brevity by plunging directly into the subject matter.

Keep Summaries to One Page

A document begins:

> This memorandum is a summary of decisions and actions up to date on the establishment of a national sales division.
> Mission:
> 1. Represent the company to large prospects whose size makes them hard for any single representative to sell.
> 2. Interface with relevant regions on pursuit of national business.

The documents rolls on, page after page. There are six items under "Mission." Then comes "Authority and Responsibility," eight items. But there's more: Personnel, Timetable, Organization, etc. All of this may be valuable information, but *it is too long for a summary*.

When a summary threatens to become too long (one page is not a bad rule of thumb), rethink it. Maybe there are too many individual items:

> Organization:
>
> national sales director
> assistant national sales director
> secretary
> four national representatives
> word-processing supervisor
> two word-processing operators

Combine items:

national sales director and assistant
four national reps with support staff

If it's appropriate, add appendixes to the summary that spell out the details—but *keep the summary short.*

If the summary contains too many main topics, do summaries on each main topic—and transmit them separately. The idea is to make the summary short and crisp, a helpful document that runs down the main points at a glance.

How Much Is Too Much?

It's always possible to get more facts about anything. Procrastinators know this very well. The need for further research is a standard excuse for delaying the decision.

It is also true that we've all got a saturation point for information. You know that you're facing an important move, and you collect as much data as possible, but the time comes (and maybe you're not even aware of it at the moment) when your appetite for facts is totally glutted. You may still go through the motions of looking at more information, but it's not registering on you, at least not with the impact that it warrants.

Keep this consideration in mind when you write a document containing a lot of facts. *Lead with the information that is most important.* This way, if your audience begins to nod, the stuff that gets missed is of relatively lesser consequence.

Break it up into more than one message if it's convenient. For example, you're writing about the restructuring of a department, a change in the department's mission, and a move in the department's location. Make it three memos instead of one.

If it all must go into one long document, *break up the parade of facts.* Write a couple of paragraphs of data. Then indent to provide some tabular material. Then put in a paragraph commenting on the implications. This approach may make the document greater in length, but because it's broken up it will read shorter.

Long Paragraphs = Instant Sominex

The following memo appears on your desk. It's important. You've got to read it. So, here goes . . .

Re: United Electric, Apparatus Sales

Apparatus Sales represents United to more than 11,000 electrical distributors throughout the United States and Canada. The distribution market enjoyed a steady growth of between 5 and 7 percent annually throughout the 1980s. Growth rate has declined to 2–3 percent within the past two years. Total market in the industry is approximately $19 billion, with more than $5 billion in the products represented by Apparatus Sales. Industry trends are towards enlargement and consolidation of outlets. Distributors serve as "supermarkets" for electrical equipment, with local financing, stocking, warehousing, distribution, and application assistance. These distributors sell to a number of industries. The construction market includes electrical and mechanical contractors engaged in major construction projects, small electrical contractors engaged in light commercial and residential construction and maintenance, and municipal public works departments. The utility market comprises municipal electrical utilities and rural cooperatives. The industrial market includes OEM . . .

And on and on like this, for three pages, *without a paragraph break*. It's numbing. The solid phalanx of print on the page defies you to keep on reading.

While this example is extreme, too many documents confront the reader with long blocks of copy so solid that they are virtually impenetrable, even to the most dedicated reader.

Sometimes this kind of thing happens because the word processor is put on automatic pilot. Whatever the reason, it shouldn't happen. Even if a long passage might qualify technically as a paragraph (because it covers only one topic), break it up anyway.

Make your document reader-friendly, in look as well as style and content.

Boosting the Signal on Long Documents

Long-distance telephone transmissions are made possible by the placement of inductance coils at intervals to reinforce the signal, which would otherwise fade in its journey through thousands of miles of wire.

You can use "inductance coils" at intervals in a long document containing a lot of minute detail. Such documents can "lose" the reader, who is unable to go the distance without reinforcement.

Provide reinforcement by inserting an occasional short paragraph that boosts the signal:

The following section covers vital elements of the plan . . .
Up to this point we have discussed objectives. Now for the people who will achieve those objectives. Staffing for the new department . . .
Here's where we are right now . . .

Insert short "breather" paragraphs to help the reader sort out the material that has already been passed along and to prepare to understand the material that is to come. These boosters will make the document a little longer, but they'll help readers to go through with more energy.

CHAPTER 9

Making the Last Word Count

Your concluding words are decisive in triggering the action you want or implanting the thought you wish to transmit. Here are some suggestions on windups that work . . .

Acknowledge the Negative Impact of Bad News

When your message is negative or contains negative elements—criticism, unwelcome change, potentially damaging developments—people think first about the effect on themselves. You can't help that, but you want them to switch their thinking into productive channels as quickly as possible:

> You will naturally have a mixture of reactions, personal as well as professional. However, I know that you'll devote your best professional efforts to making an objective assessment and beginning to build a plan based on that assessment.

Shape the Next Move with a Question

You can influence the way readers think about a document by winding up with a well-chosen question. Here are some windup questions designed to shape reaction and direct the next steps:

> How can we use these facts to build a plan to increase market share?
> Would you give me your reaction in terms of impact on organizational planning?
> How do you intend to capitalize on the development?
> When will you have a comprehensive answer?
> How seriously should we take this news?
> Which element, in your opinion, is most significant?

"Don't Call Me . . ."

Having delivered your message, you want this to be the end of it for the time being. You don't want a reply that raises more questions, offers more rebuttals, picks more nits. The subject doesn't have to be closed permanently. You want it to be closed until you choose to reopen it.

In other words, "Don't call me; I'll call you." You can't say that in so many words. So you wind up in a way that gives the reader a sense of accomplishment while keeping the option for the next move in your hands:

> We've accomplished a lot on this matter, even though there will be more to do in the future. Thanks for all you've done. You'll be hearing from me about the next steps when it's time to discuss them.

Set Ground Rules for What Happens Next

You want people to be free to use their own initiative in responding to your message. However, there are certain directions in which you don't want them to go. Open the door to ideas, but set ground rules:

> This is a challenge to our strength and flexibility as an organization. We need to come up with fresh and workable strategies that don't involve additional point-of-purchase advertising or couponing. I look forward to hearing from you.

Offer a Suggestion

You want the recipient of your message to react in a certain way, but you're not in a position to issue a flat-out direction. Instead, offer a leading suggestion:

> We're ready to take the next steps as soon as we hear from you. One possibility that occurs to me is that we might cut our processing time by as much as a week by networking directly between the foreign branches and headquarters. Should you want more input on how this could be done, we'll provide it.

Point the Reader in the Right Direction

Where appropriate, you can do the reader a favor by indicating a direction without actually issuing an order, particularly when your subordinates may be sitting there wondering exactly what you mean and what you want.

> Given the situation as I've outlined it, I'm sure you'll want to rethink the job descriptions within your department, with an eye toward handling a broader range of responsibilities without adding to staff.

Tell the Reader What to Expect Next

"What happens next?" This may be the question your message leaves in the reader's mind. When it's possible (and helpful), answer it:

As a result of these changes, you will see a consolidation of deliveries, beginning June 15. You will receive one or two shipments a month, rather than four to six.

Skip Banal Conclusions

A writer sends a clear, urgent message to another department. The memo describes a potentially dangerous situation that the recipient should act on right away. Then the memo concludes:

I hope this matter will receive your immediate attention.

Endings like this tend to trivialize the message. Of course the writer hopes the matter will receive immediate attention—or that the reader will "get back to me at your earliest convenience" or "take the foregoing under advisement."

If you want specific action, spell it out: "Call me as soon as you've read this." If the message speaks for itself, don't add a trite flourish.

Use "Banal" Endings That Have a Function

Although you shouldn't use the trite endings discussed in the preceding section, there are times when one of these seemingly banal windups conveys a subtle message—one you want to convey.

For example, an executive has been queried by a superior about some hard-to-collect data. The executive takes the time and effort to come up with the answers. The answers are written *at full length;* the writer includes every fact. Then she winds up:

We are confident that this answers all your questions.

Ordinarily this would be a meaningless sentence. Here, however, it conveys the message that the numbers took a lot of effort to put together and that the writer hopes this is the end of it.

In the same way, the conventional "give me a call" ending can be used to put the ball in the recipient's court. The writer wants the recipient to handle a problem on his own. However, the writer doesn't want to leave the reader out on a limb. If the other guy really needs more help, he should feel he can get it. The writer doesn't want to seem too eager for further exchange, so he doesn't write:

> Please get in touch so we can discuss this further.

Instead, the windup is more formal with less oomph:

> Give me a call if I can be of any further help.

End with a Forcing Question

It's appropriate to end some documents with a question. Often those questions are stereotyped:

> Will you be good enough to forward the requested material?
> May I expect your immediate attention?
> Can we be of further service?

The question ending can be an effective way of impelling the reader toward the next step. Instead of *pro forma* questions, which lose impact because of their familiarity and stiffness, use conversational questions with more freshness and vigor:

> Can you give me what I need right away?
> What's your next move?
> Will I be hearing from you this week?
> What else can we do to move the process along?

CHAPTER 10

Political Ploys and Dirty Tricks

They don't give courses in company politics at business school. The American Management Association does not conduct seminars on how to outmaneuver your rivals for promotion. The techniques of intrigue and infighting are learned in the jungle. Some learn faster than others. The slower learners don't survive.

You need more than excellence to make it. You need to be able to make your excellence shine brighter than the others'. We live in the age of PR. Public relations is a central factor in the making of presidents, the disposition of billions, and the resolution of great issues. It helps to have right and logic on your side. It also helps to be able to engineer the perception of those whose judgment affects your fate.

Self-packaging, therefore, is a key element in personal success. In a broad sense, everything in this book is aimed at helping you to package yourself better. A lot of what you write is important in reflecting an image of you as well as in accomplishing its primary purpose of informing, responding, analyzing, and so on.

Sometimes, in the arena of corporate politics, you need to use words as very sharp tools—to defend yourself, to delay when delay is your best tactic, to put a rival on the defensive, to maximize your assets and minimize your liabilities. More and more, these infighting words are *written* words. The reality game of company politics is played on paper or computer screens.

This chapter gives you a selection of writing ploys (some of them pretty dirty) to help you survive in the jungle.

If You're Lying, Don't Elaborate

Many years ago a British aristocrat received an invitation he did not wish to accept. He had no valid excuse for refusing. The usual practice was to send a telegram: "Sorry, cannot attend. Explanation follows by mail." A follow-up letter would spin out an elaborate excuse.

This nobleman flouted the convention. He wired: "Cannot come. Lie follows by mail."

We all tell "convenience lies": "Sorry, I'm going into a meeting"; "I'm all tied up that day"; and so on. By and large, others accept these excuses without looking into them too closely.

Occasionally it's necessary to use an evasion or outright lie in writing. When they face the necessity to put untruths in black and white, some people feel squeamish. As a result, they overelaborate:

> I'm sorry to have to withdraw from your conference. Jim Wilson, our West Coast manager, is coming to HQ that week. I need to work with Jim on the upcoming budget. His schedule doesn't permit . . .

The writer "doth protest too much." Just make the excuse:

> Because of a conflict, I won't be able to attend your conference . . .

Giving Your Rivals Full Credit in Print

A competitor within the company has made a mistake. You'd be less than human if you didn't feel a little gratified. You might even be tempted to gloat a little.

Do your gloating, if you must, during conversations with people who are very close to you. When it comes to writing, the smart thing to do is lean over backward to be fair, understanding—even favorable—to your rival.

Here's the sort of thing to avoid:

> George's overestimation of the preproduction time on the new model was potentially very damaging. We were able to handle the problem, but the implications of this kind of judgment are alarming for the future . . .

The writer would have done better with this:

> We all agree that we should develop safeguards against this kind of miscalculation. It's possible that something similar could happen within the bailiwicks of any of us. Let's meet to talk about a review mechanism . . .

When a rival has stumbled, don't stick it to the guy in print. You're apt to look bad. Be constructive, understanding, even supportive. Not only does it make you look better, but it's also better for the cohesiveness and effectiveness of the organization.

Calculated Ambiguity

You're being pressured for answers that you're not quite ready to give. You need to buy a little time. This is the moment to abandon the golden rule of clarity. Use *calculated ambiguity* to comply with the requirement for an answer while leaving yourself some room to maneuver.

Politicians are masters of calculated ambiguity. Take this statement by an official who was asked if reorganization of a state agency would mean higher taxes:

> The answer is quite direct. Reorganization will be completed within the present revenue structure with one focus of attention directed at more cost effectiveness and more services for the same tax dollar.

Blur the language a little. Emphasize at least one point on which everyone can agree. For example, you're asked if a specific project will be completed by a specific date. You might respond:

> Completion of this project is assured within the time frame envisioned at the project's inception.

Warning. Ambiguity is a short-term holding action. *Get the answers and provide them quickly.*

Spreading the Liability

You've been asked to make recommendations on a very sensitive topic—which of two competing divisions should be assigned a new product development project. The ultimate decision will be made by the executive vice-president. He has given you the task of studying the matter and coming down on one side or the other.

It's a mixed blessing. It's nice to inspire enough confidence to get such an assignment. But it's a hot potato. Whichever side loses, the loser will resent the person who was influential in the decision.

You could come back with a noncommittal answer: "There are merits on both sides . . ." That would be wimpy and unproductive. You could be political and slant your recommendation toward the side whose victory would do you the most good. That would be cynical and self-serving.

Give it your best shot and make a definite, objective recommendation. But minimize, to the extent possible, the fallout. After stating your conclusion clearly, support your argument, not only with objective facts, but also with quotes from various senior officials. Put them on record along with you. And make it clear that you were carrying out an assignment.

Here's how such a report might start:

You asked me to make a thorough and objective investigation of the question as to assignment of the Planetary Project.

I have looked at all the relevant data, inside and outside the company, and spoken with the following people:

[Name the "influentials" you talked to, even if they did not all contribute decisively to your decision.]

My recommendation is that the project be assigned to Domestic Services, for the following reasons:

[As you give your reasons, quote the agreement of others. At the same time, put in quotations from those who leaned in the other direction.]

Now you're in the position of someone who did a thorough job of putting together data and opinion to come to a logical conclusion, rather than somebody who pretty much made the decision on your own.

When you're called upon to go on record with something that can make you a target, it makes sense to surround yourself (in print) with allies.

Putting the Ball in the Other Guy's Court

In a perfect world there would be no need for delaying tactics. As a practical matter, you occasionally need a way of stalling when you're up against a deadline without being quite prepared to meet it.

One way to give yourself a little extra time is to shift the obligation for the next move to the other person.

You're scheduled to send a comprehensive report by a certain date. You've got most of the data but not all. The deadline is still a few days away, but it's obvious you can't make it. Here's how you might handle it:

This progress report will bring you up to date on the Project Pluto report.

Principal findings so far:

[Describe in brief the most interesting aspects of your research.]

As you probably see, these developments suggest another avenue that might be explored, beyond the scope of the task as you outlined it.

[Describe a logical extension of the assignment that could be undertaken if the other party agrees.]

Please let me know if you want the report expanded to cover this aspect.

You haven't asked for a delay, nor have you said you're having trouble meeting the deadline. You have raised the possibility of broadening the report. Implicit in this question is the assumption that the deadline would have to be changed.

And you have put the ball in the other guy's court. The recipient may agree that the report should be expanded and the deadline extended. Or you may be instructed to stick to the confines of the original assignment. In either case it may take some time to get a reply.

Stalling is never a preferred tactic. This approach is recommended only when you have little choice. Its virtue is that the deadline extension would be a by-product of your initiative rather than an admission of inadequacy.

Sharing the Responsibility

Let's face it. Office politics is a fact of life. And part of office politics is getting the other guy to bear the responsibility for failure.

When it looks as if you're the target and you're going to get stuck with more than your share of the blame, restore the balance by getting on record with a document that tells how others played their parts in the action. Obviously this is not the ostensible purpose of the document. Make it a roundup or overview of the situation:

Here's an update on the Clovis matter.
   Following the directive sent by George Wilson on August 9, I spoke with Charlie Agajanian. On August 12, I authorized the revised deal. As Helen McMahon indicated in her critique, this "appears to be the best course available to us" . . .

The people you name will know what you're doing. That's not your concern. Your concern is to be on record when, on the Olympian heights, the top brass sits down to review the case and figure out what went wrong and who's responsible.

By keeping files and quoting others to good effect you can protect your rear while seeming to make an earnest contribution to the exchange of ideas.

Defusing Criticism by Exaggerating It

Many office intriguers prefer sniping to direct confrontation. They use written messages to make damaging references to rivals. The criticism is usually indirect, as in the following excerpt:

An overview of progress so far shows that most divisions are on track or close to it. The one major exception is Central, which is showing volume increases at a lower rate than the average of the rest of the country. Andy Gross has listed

some persuasive reasons for Central's performance, and he states that he
hopes for better results by year's end . . .

This veiled condemnation of Andy Gross (by a rival) is meant to make the
CEO think Gross is not pulling his weight. In truth, Gross's Central Division
is on track. "Volume increases at a lower rate" was predicted and meets the
budget.

Gross has several ways of dealing with this memo. He can ignore it,
figuring that those close to the situation know the truth of the matter. The
trouble with this nonresponse is that senior executives of the company may
not know all the details and may be left (as the writer intended) with the
impression of less than good performance by Gross.

Another choice would be to write a memo minimizing the criticism and
trying to put it in its proper perspective. Gross prefers not to make a defensive
response.

He chooses a more novel answer. He writes a memo which appears to take
the criticism *very seriously indeed:*

Rick's overview memo seems to indicate that he has identified some problems
in Central that we have overlooked. He notes that our volume increase is lower
than the rest of the country. While that was expected (because of the severe and
special problems affecting Central), we don't want to use that as an excuse for
anything we may be doing wrong.
    Therefore, I have invited Rick to meet with us as soon as possible to discuss
his criticisms and to hear his recommendations . . .

When an office politician writes a memo that makes you look bad, think
about calling the bluff. The critic, confronted with the challenge to put up or
shut up, can be made to look petty and self-seeking.

Such a tactic also has the advantage of keeping company correspondence
focused on company matters, not personal ambition.

Raising Questions about a Rival with Vague Cautions

Fights for promotion are unfortunate and lamentable. They waste a lot of
time and energy that could be used more productively. They damage cooperation.

But they also bring out some creative tactics.

Like the "faint alarm bell" tactic. Here's how one manager uses it. When
a competitor writes to describe a new plan or convey a new idea, the manager
doesn't engage in direct criticism unless there is something that is clearly

vulnerable to criticism. Instead he praises the plan and agrees with it—while sticking in a little comment here and there designed to create doubts:

> The program as outlined seems well designed to fit the situation. Phase II is particularly innovative. (I assume Legal has said it's okay.)

The writer knows the word "innovative" is a little scary to some of the organization's senior management. Moreover, he knows perfectly well that the legal department hasn't looked it over. He is reasonably sure that, if the idea is submitted to them at this stage, the attorneys will take a long time to look at it—and then find at least one thing that should be changed. That's the way most legal departments work.

So just the mention of a possibility that there may be a legal problem is enough to cool the enthusiasm of top management and dim the luster of the idea.

"Seeding" Your Data to Trap a Thief

Some people habitually steal the work of others and present it as their own. In the direct mail business there's a protection against this kind of larceny. It's called seeding. To protect lists from unauthorized use, the proprietors "seed" the lists with phony names and addresses. When the thieves use the lists, they send mailings to these planted addressees. The proprietor can then use the mailings as proof against claims that the bandit compiled the list independently.

Here's an extreme use of the principle in handling somebody who uses data developed by others without giving proper credit. "Can I look over your figures on the Wilson deal?" asks a notorious data robber. The person who worked hard to develop the figures passes them along. Soon the figures are incorporated into an authoritative-sounding report sent out by the thief (who neglects to mention the originator).

Then comes the embarrassing truth. There is an egregious error in the figures. The thief, relying on the accuracy of the originator, hasn't checked them out properly. The robber has to explain the error. The originator says, innocently, "Gee, I just thought you were going to look it over, so I gave you my raw notes."

Tough.

Giving a Rival Credit for Something He *Didn't* Do

The manager of a department sends—to a wide audience—a memo describing the successful completion of a difficult project. The manager of another department responds:

> Joe's description of this achievement interested me greatly. There is a great
> deal to praise here—especially in light of the fact that Joe was able to keep
> overtime charges at or below last year's levels.

It happens that Joe did *not* keep overtime at last year's levels. In fact,
overtime was quite high. Joe did not mention it in his jubilant report. Maybe
this issue is not all that important in the light of the accomplishment, but Joe
will now have to acknowledge the fact.

When asked to explain his comment about Joe's control of overtime, the
writer answers, ''Since there was no mention of higher overtime, I naturally
assumed that it was okay.''

Putting Doubts in the Other Person's Mind

You are required to comment on a proposal. It looks good. All the elements
hang together. The writer of the proposal seems to have done his homework.

And yet you have nagging doubts. Your doubts are not specific enough to
warrant disagreement, but there is one element of the proposition that bothers
you. Though you don't want to make a big deal of it, you don't want to go on
record as accepting it without question.

So you cast a doubt on the questionable area. In the middle of a generally
favorable critique, you stick in your qualifying words:

> Everything about this loan seems to be proceeding on track. The executed
> commitment is in order, and the borrower's council has been properly briefed. I
> was a little surprised to note that Higeshima will be able to purchase a $40M
> participation, but other than that . . .

''*I was a little surprised . . .*'' It doesn't exactly mean anything, and yet
it can indicate that you have some free-floating doubts that are not specific
enough to make you disagree.

When You Win by Saying "I Don't Know"

People who try to exaggerate their knowledge often get into trouble. And
yet the tendency to claim expertise is widespread.

Instead of exaggerating your knowledge, you can score points by *under-
playing* what you know about a particular situation. For example, the company
is thinking of opening a branch in San Jose. People are vying to emphasize
their qualifications to run the operation. One competitor, anxious to present
an image of expertise, writes along these lines:

I have developed considerable feel for that area. San Jose, with its metropolitan area of 1.3 million, is a focal point, at the base of the San Mateo peninsula and looking south toward the growing Monterey market area . . .

The document goes on with a lot of stuff that looks as if it were hastily dug out of reference books.

Another competitor takes a different tack:

I'm afraid I don't know much about San Jose. It's been more than two years since I spent more than a couple of days there. I do recall Jane Morgan, top honcho in the C of C, briefing me on how the city is an altogether different selling proposition from San Francisco. A few things I noted . . .

When you start by admitting ignorance, then follow up with nuggets of information and experience, you make the most of what you know. You haven't claimed to be an expert, so you're not held up to the highest standard. And you get credit for modesty.

Attacking the Enemy's Strongest Point

The immortal Stephen Potter, patron saint of one-upmanship, suggested that literary critics could cut an author down to size by attacking the single quality for which the writer is most famous: "Mickey Spillane's prudish reticence about sex and violence."

Potter's principle can be useful in political infighting. A rival sends out a lengthy document. The rival may be short on imagination and guts, but he is methodical to the *n*th degree, researching everything exhaustively. The long report is typical—pages and pages of numbers, tables, appendixes, and so on.

Attack at the strongest point. No matter how complete the research may be, it must leave something out. Locate what is lacking. Then write:

Jim's research skims over a few points. (The analysis of commodity prices extends back no more than ten years.) Nevertheless his report is a valuable contribution, which suggests some new directions in which our thinking should go.

"Thanks a Lot!"

A rival sends you a communication (which you did not ask for), making some "helpful" comments on a situation within your department. The rival has, of course, sent FYI copies to all of the top brass in the company.

What to do? It would not look good to tell the guy to mind his own damn business—at least, it would not look good on paper. Nor should you nitpick the contribution, or get into a dispute about it.

Thank the helpful associate in a way that tends to diminish the value of the contribution, cast doubt on the motives of the contributor, and emphasize your own resourcefulness and command of the situation. Send your thanks with copies to the same list:

Thanks for taking time away from struggling with your overtime situation to think about our productivity program. You have summed up what we're doing very well. Your comments have helped me to focus on one or two new aspects of the program. When we put the finishing touches on these concepts, I think we can express our gratitude to you by providing some approaches that you'll find helpful. . . .

When Things Go Worse Than Expected

Your project is not going well. It's not a total disaster, but results are disappointing. Now you have to put out a report. You can't sugarcoat the news, but you can put it in perspective.

One method you might use is to show how much worse it might be:

Results so far have led us to take a hard look at the downside risk for this project. This task is never fun, but it's our responsibility to be realistic. Extrapolating to the end of the year, the worst-case scenario would be a loss of share exceeding 5 percent.

Our best estimate is that the worst will not happen. The share loss will be on the order of 2–3 percent. The key indicators underpinning this projection are . . .

When Things Go Better Than Expected

Your project is exceeding expectations. Some people would brag about such results. Instead of being smug, underplay your success. Show that you're not smug and that you have no inclination to coast. Focus on the things you still intend to accomplish:

We're pleased that it has gone this well. Actually we're not surprised. While the tangible obstacles were quite large, we know about our "intangibles"—our resourcefulness and experience. So we don't see this as that much of a triumph. In fact, I believe we could have done better on signing up new distributors, and we're concentrating on that area for next quarter. . . .

How to Explain What Went Wrong

When you have to write a report of failure, you may be tempted to

- minimize the failure.
- spread the responsibility.
- find excuses for what went wrong.

You may be able to do yourself a lot of good by doing none of these things. Instead of weaseling, take *more* of the blame than is fair:

> While it would be possible to throw up a smokescreen of alibis, the bottom line is that I blew it. I overestimated our ability to penetrate the midlevel market and did not anticipate the speed with which competition would respond . . .

Having taken the blame, the writer continues with a factual explanation. As the details emerge, it becomes clear that the blame can—and should—be shared by others. The manager was not supported by adequate research, production made promises that were not fulfilled, and so on. The reader is led to conclude that the writer has assumed too much personal responsibility.

It's always better to be perceived as having the guts to take the heat than to be regarded as someone who spreads the onus to others.

Hedging a Prediction—Tell Why It May Go Wrong

Some people in business try to project an aura of omniscience. This can be an effective strategy in personal PR, but it doesn't work if the person's predictions are unambiguous and subject to scrutiny. Since no human is infallible, some forecasts are bound to go awry.

Such considerations will not stop certain people from trying to make you the fall guy when one of your predictions fails to pan out. When making forecasts, you want—as far as possible—to protect yourself against this possibility. One way to do so is to *admit that you're human and fallible—and even exaggerate your potential for being wrong.*

After making your forecast, discuss the factors that may make things turn out otherwise. Don't minimize these factors; if anything, build them up:

> This projection could turn out to be too high by as much as 14 percent if McCullers, our chief competitor, brings out a new product within six months . . .

The fact is that the writer has a strong suspicion that the competitor *will* bring out the new product within six months, but that this eventuality would not affect the forecast all that much.

Responding to a Cheap Shot

A rival has criticized you unfairly and inaccurately. Here's your chance to rip him apart. You can blow him out of the water by scornfully exposing the invalidity of the criticism and questioning the motives for making it.

But let's hold on a second. You may be able to make a far more effective response by *seeming to take the criticism more seriously than it deserves.* Repeat the criticism. Then provide an objective analysis of it:

> George states that our operation has consistently overstated performance and understated costs, sometimes to a very great extent.
>
> If George's observations were true, it would indicate some critical problems in the way we work. So we took the following steps to look into the situation. First, I appointed a task force . . .

The memo goes on to spell out, dispassionately, a series of moves. Then the result:

> We were able to reassure George that there is no validity to these speculations. The episode did give us the opportunity, which we always welcome, to examine ourselves objectively. And, in fact, while George's fears were not borne out, we have instituted a couple of procedures that will strengthen our assessment and reporting . . .

The originator of a cheap shot is made to look even worse when you respond, not in anger or scorn, but with a low-key, factual refutation.

Putting a Rival on the Spot with an Extravagant Compliment

When a competitor for advancement scores an unmistakable success, you don't want to appear grudging or small-minded. Your reaction should acknowledge the coup gracefully.

In fact, you can put your rival on the spot by making your compliments so extravagant as to increase the load of expectation on his shoulders:

> Roger's pride in having solved this problem is understandable and thoroughly justified. It's a genuine accomplishment. Its greatest significance is what it promises for the future. Under the new setup, the division will undoubtedly show a substantial improvement in bottom-line performance . . .

The writer is not damning with faint praise, but rather raising the stakes—and the pressure—with lavish praise.

Lowering Expectations in the Wake of a Success

When you score a success, people expect more of you next time. "What have you done for us lately?" is the keynote. Even if you do very well the next time, if you fall short of an absolute smash you may look as if you're losing it.

So when you announce a success, think about the future. You're entitled to be proud of what you've done, but you may want to put in some words designed to lower expectations somewhat. This tactic is especially important when you're trying to cope with adroit rivals who may use your success to build expectations to a level that you can't reach next time.

So qualify the success:

We were able to achieve results of this magnitude because a number of factors—some of them out of our control—came together at just the right time. We're well aware that we can't expect everything to coalesce perfectly like this again, so we are guarding against false optimism or unreasonable expectations.

"Blind" Quotation—A Trap for the Unwary

When you're contending with a rival who nitpicks your memos, you need ways to strike back. One way is by use of a "blind" quotation—an unattributed quote unfamiliar to the rival but very familiar to a top executive who will also be reading the document.

Here's how one young manager used the ploy. She had been criticized several times by a more experienced colleague (and political adversary). The adversary loved to shoot holes in her logic. The strife went on under the scrutiny of the company's president and COO, who received FYI copies of the correspondence.

So the beleaguered manager wrote, as part of a memo:

Goal achievement is a valuable concept, but it is not the be-all and end-all of motivation. After all, "We have to admit that a lot of jobs, including supervisory and even management jobs, are done by rote." For people in these jobs, goal awareness is the better approach to building morale and reducing absenteeism.

As the writer hoped, the nitpicking colleague jumped on the unattributed quote: "Maggie doesn't indicate who said this, but I think we can agree it's a shortsighted viewpoint." Short-sighted it may be, but the quotation happened to be uttered by the president and COO. The often-criticized manager recorded the quote and used it deliberately without attribution. The critical colleague, whose specialty is currying favor, has been lured into knocking the boss.

Refuting the Assertions of Another

Someone has written a document with which you disagree. You want to write a refutation. What's the best way to organize it?

If your quarrel is with just one part of the other document, start by indicating the points of agreement:

I agree with Marty's points 1, 2, 3, 5, and 7. I have problems with points 4 and 6.

Then take up the questionable points individually.

When you disagree totally with a document, it's not enough just to reject it. Take up each point, summarize it briefly, and then tell why you disagree:

Following up leads—Marty says leads should be evaluated and screened before being sent to the field. In my judgment, there is a key question: *Who does the screening?* Sales HQ staff lacks the knowledge and expertise to screen these leads accurately . . .

Hedge Words

The meeting has been a snakepit of political maneuvering among several rivals for advancement. The subject under discussion is a hot potato. Anyone who takes a firm position on it, right or wrong, is a target. At the end of the meeting, in one of those sudden coalitions, the others have all banded together and agreed that you write the report on the dangerous topic.

You know your research will be imperfect because there is just not enough information available now. And you know your conclusions are apt to be controversial. Whichever side you come down on, you're going to make some influential people unhappy.

You could try to play it down the middle, turning out a report that doesn't really say anything. Or you could ask for more time. Either way you're in danger of looking like a wimp.

Here's a better way to do it. Put together the data available. Draw the best conclusions you can. Then start off by using a hedging mechanism:

To conclude our spirited discussion of December 9, I took on the job of preparing an interim report. This preliminary study includes tentative conclusions advanced as debating points.

Putting Your Rivals on the Spot

When you have been put on the spot by being assigned to turn out a document on a controversial subject, you want to do several things. You want to do the best job you can of covering the topic. You want to protect yourself. And, if possible, you want to turn some of the heat toward your rivals.

We've talked about *hedge words* like "preliminary" or "interim." They enable you to position your document as an important step in an evolutionary process.

You can smoke out the stands of others on the hot topic by using strategic questions. After laying out the facts and advancing your tentative conclusions, write something like this:

> These are the facts as I see them now. For discussion purposes I have been willing to draw some inferences and advance some tentative conclusions.
>
> Here are a few suggestions as to how we can move this process ahead. I suggest that you all respond to these questions:
>
> - Do you disagree specifically with any point or points in the overview section?
> - Do you agree with the preliminary findings?
> - If not, how and why do you disagree?
>
> In particular, I know Jerry will want to take a stand, as he has been most forceful in driving home the urgency of the decision.

Targeted Segment

The targeted segment is a portion of a document that is clear to one addressee but not clear to other addressees.

This is strictly a political ploy. Normally the idea is to make all parts of the document clear to everybody who reads it. In a perfect world you would always strive for universal clarity. Unfortunately, in this imperfect world there is office politics, and rivals may sometimes play political games to win favor with the boss and make you look bad.

One way to strike back is with the targeted segment. For example:

> In its effort to win a higher budget allocation, R&D seems to be adopting the "PITA Principle."

Most recipients of the memo containing this sentence are ignorant of the meaning of "PITA Principle." The writer doesn't help them out by defining the term. He knows that the CEO, an information addressee, used the words recently in a fit of irritation. (PITA means "pain in the ass.")

The writer hopes the CEO will recognize the term and acknowledge the writer's alertness and wit in using it. Others will have to ask for the meaning or remain in the dark.

Questions That Raise Doubts

Office politics involves a variety of ploys. One ploy is to keep rivals off balance.

Let's say an adversary has sent out a triumphant message, announcing the acquisition of a new customer. You send a quick and graceful note (with copies to the appropriate places):

Congratulations on the Billingsgate account. Billingsgate has always had a lot to recommend it. I assume their credit situation has cleared up now so we can have a profitable relationship with them.

Since no company is perfect, it's usually safe to refer to a ''credit situation'' or some other ''situation.''

CHAPTER 11

Rules: When to Follow Them, When to Break Them

Good writers are comfortable enough with the rules of grammar to violate those rules to achieve special effects. This chapter hits the high spots on the Rules of the Game. Grammar and syntax. Word selection. Sentence structure. It's not a complete text on usage, punctuation, and the like. (A good book on usage should be part of your reference library.) Here we spotlight some of the most important and most frequently violated rules.

Here too you will find suggestions on *when and how to break the rules*.

It's risky to break the rules. Treading the beaten path is the safe way to go. But adroit risk taking is a paramount attribute of the successful executive.

You can score with great impact by smashing an established rule of writing, by writing nonsentences, by using words not ordinarily seen in polite use, by committing deliberate grammatical sins to open the eyes and nail the attention of the reader.

So here are some rules you should follow—and some rules you should break.

Breaking the Rules—"He" or "Him"

When certain pronouns are used as objects they can look unnatural, even affected:

Will Jane or he be hired, do you think?
The culprit, it turned out, was he.
Sandy writes better than I.
Virgil Soames is the candidate whom we hope to elect.

These examples, all from *The Elements of Style* (third edition, Macmillan, 1979, pp. 11–12), by William Strunk, Jr., and E. B. White, are grammatically correct. But writers who write this way run the risk of appearing ridiculous. Using "he" instead of "him," "I" instead of "me," "who" instead of "whom"—well, correctness can have too high a price.

Avoid the problem where you can:

> He turned out to be the culprit.
> We hope to elect Virgil Soames.
> I don't write as well as Sandy.

When there isn't a convenient way to avoid the problem, pick the more common usage over the book-correct one:

> Who will we appoint?

Deliberate Mistakes

Pogo's saying "We have met the enemy, and it is us" would be far less memorable if the cartoonist Walt Kelly had written, "We have met the enemy, and they are identical to ourselves."

There are moments when a calculated lapse from proper form gives impact to your message. However, this is a tricky tactic. The lapse must not be just slangy and trite:

> They want us to open our books. We ain't going to do it.

The lapse has to be clearly deliberate. Otherwise, the writer may seem ignorant of the rules of grammar:

> Don't anybody know how to do things right around here?

Use the deliberate mistake in specialized cases. You have to know your audience. And you must use the calculated lapse in such a way that it can't be misinterpreted as mere carelessness.

Having mentioned these qualifications, we repeat that, used adroitly, this tactic can convey a message in earthy and conversational fashion. One good ploy is to use a grammatical quirk that the reader has heard you use in speaking:

> We will not ease credit arrangements with this class of customer under any circumstances, no way, nohow.

It's a Sin to "Ly"

> Firstly, the term of membership on the board should be increased from three to seven years. Secondly, the mandatory retirement age should be eliminated. Thirdly, there must be a mechanism for evaluating performance. Fourthly, there should be provision for removing ineffective or nonperforming board members.

This excerpt is an example of the "ly" fallacy in action. Technically, it is true that addition of "ly" turns an adjective (first) into an adverb. But it's cumbersome and unnecessary. Whenever you're tempted to append "ly" to a word, see how it looks without the addition:

First, the term of membership . .

Notoriety Is Not Nice

After just two weeks, our InterAction Program has achieved great notoriety in the community.

The author of this line means that a lot of people know about the program, and that this is a good thing. "Notoriety" is frequently used this way. But "notoriety" means "the state of being notorious." Notorious means widely known; but usually it is taken to mean *unfavorably* known. Tylenol is a well-known product. It became *notorious* after the poisoning episode. A lot of good thinking and hard work went into overcoming that notoriety.

So, unless you want to say something is notorious, don't say it has notoriety. Use another term: *familiar, well-known, famous, noted.*

Flaunt It, Don't Flout It

Some words get mixed up because they look alike.
For example, it's not uncommon to see usages like the following:

By pursuing this approach, the sales department is flaunting long-standing company policy on the granting of exclusive franchises.

"Flaunt" means to wave or display something; to show off proudly or defiantly. But "flaunt" is often used to mean "flout"—which means to mock, scorn, or show contempt for something:

Congress has once again flaunted the Constitution.

Even *The Wall Street Journal* has been known to fall into the flaunt/flout trap. (Incidentally, it doesn't work the other way. When people wave a banner defiantly, they are not described as "flouting" it.)

Don't use "flaunt" when you mean "flout." You may not want to use "flout" either. Although it's a fine old word, it's a bit archaic for business correspondence. Look for another word: *defy, disregard, ignore, ridicule.*

Factoring Out "Factor"

We all know that two or three words are not more impressive than one word, but sometimes document writers act as if several words add weight to the message.

This mistake is often made when the word "factor" is used.

We advise you to be cautious about the backlash factor.
The competitive factor is important in deciding . . .
I'm concerned about the morale factor . . .

"Factor" weakens these sentences:

Watch out for backlash.
Competition is important . . .
I'm concerned about morale . . .

When you're tempted to use "factor," stop and think about the shorter word that could be used in its place. (There will almost always be one.)

When to Put the Conclusion at the Beginning

When you read a mystery story, you expect the conclusion to come at the end. If the author told you in the first paragraph that "the butler did it," you'd skip the rest of the story.

Some people write a recommendation memo as if it were a whodunit. They state the topic, describe the situation, sum up the factors pro and con, and then disclose what they think.

This approach may build suspense, but it wastes time. Often the recipient has to read the document again to learn how the writer supports the conclusion.

Put the "ending" at the beginning:

We should expand the Omaha facility rather than building a new facility in Denver.

Go on to tell why.

Leave the suspense to Sherlock Holmes. State your conclusion first, then explain it.

When It's All Right to Run On, and On, and On . . .

One of the villains we meet in elementary English is the "run-on sentence." The run-on sentence is two or more sentences basted together loosely by commas:

We received the bid, we confirmed it with the vendor, we submitted it to the evaluation procedure.

You learn early in life to break such a construction into separate sentences. Or we rework the sentence:

We received the bid, confirmed it, and submitted it to the evaluation process.

But there are times when even the despised run-on sentence can be used to make a point. Let's say the writer is trying to emphasize the cumbersomeness of a needlessly complex process:

We received the bid, we circulated copies, we confirmed it with the vendor, we put it on the agenda, we passed out the supporting material, etc., etc. . . . And this was only the beginning of the process!

Some things in business run on too long. You can use a run-on sentence to parody them.

Cut Down Your Quota of Quotes

Have you ever noticed how some local businesses scatter quotation marks over advertising copy like sprinkles on an ice cream cone?

On signs and in the Yellow Pages you'll find:

"Statewide Coverage"
"Serving Leadville for Thirty Years"
"Everything at Low Low Prices"
"The Most Respected Name in Hair Replacement"

Unnecessary quotation marks look funny and seem to cast doubt upon the words they contain.

Some business writers use quotation marks around informal expressions:

The distance is forty miles "as the crow flies."
His suggestion came "out of left field."
I think you have "hit the nail on the head."

As we discuss elsewhere, slang and colloquialisms are effective when used in the right place. When you use them, write them in the ordinary way. Putting quotes around them makes it look as if you're uncomfortable with what you've written.

Use informal language when it works. Don't apologize for it by placing it in quotes.

Watch Your "As"

Sentences beginning with "as" run the risk of a dangling construction:

As outlined in the policy memo 66, all brand managers will receive weekly field reports.

The brand managers were not outlined in the memo. It should read:

As outlined in policy memo 66, the new procedure requires all brand managers will receive call reports.

The sentence works better when it's restructured to avoid the opening "as":

In conformity with policy memo 66, all brand managers . . .

Using Parentheses or Dashes

Commas are the least intrusive punctuation marks. They cause a slight jog in the sentence rather than bringing it to a stop. Writers seeking flowing prose prefer commas to colons, semicolons, and other marks.

Occasionally you can be tripped up by reliance on just commas:

During this period the association has contributed to the growth of advertising and public relations, its main areas of concentration, as well as the overall communications sector.

"Its main areas of concentration" modifies the phrase that precedes it. Commas do not make this relationship clear. Use parentheses:

During this period the association has contributed to the growth of advertising and public relations (its main areas of concern) as well as . . .

Or use dashes, which some writers favor because they seem to provide a staccato energy:

During this period the association has contributed to the growth of advertising and public relations—its main areas of concern—as well as . . .

Prepositions: Skip Them When They're Not Necessary

Conventional usage requires that prepositions be repeated each time the sentence contains connected elements:

They will sell this equipment to us and to anyone else who meets their price.

Sometimes such repetition may seem a little stilted:

I'll be meeting with Accounts Receivable and with Accounts Payable at two different times.

If you feel such a construction is a little artificial, drop the second preposition:

I'll be meeting with Accounts Receivable and Accounts Payable at two different times.

It depends on the tone you want to set. Meticulous insertion of all the required pronouns confers formality; leaving out the second preposition when the omission doesn't blur the meaning is more conversational.

Ending with a Preposition: Nothing to Apologize for

Time was that ending a sentence with a preposition was a major no-no. Writers would go through contortions to avoid the offense:

About what topics do you want me to speak?

Nowadays it's okay to be more relaxed:

What do you want me to speak about?

If you use good sentence structure, you won't run into too many instances of prepositional endings. When they come up, and they're natural, don't worry about it:

There's nothing in their revised presentation that we have to respond to.

"Is When"—Maybe You Can Say It, but Don't Write It

We occasionally use corruptions of grammar in ordinary speech because they're informal and easy to say and because everybody understands them. Here's one: Iatrogenic intervention is when the medical treatment makes the sickness worse.

Spoken, that can sound exactly right. Avoid the usage in writing. On the screen or on the page it is jarring. Change the sentence:

When medical treatment makes the sickness worse, the development is called iatrogenic intervention.

Who Is It Happening to?

Crisp writers don't spell everything out in complete detail. They save time and space by omitting the things that are obvious.

That last sentence is an example. If the sentence were completely finished off it would read:

They save time and space by omitting the things that are obvious <u>to the reader.</u>

Sometimes, however, failure to finish off the thought leads to uncertainty:

At present they are maintaining the arrangement with their prime contractors under the existing terms. This arrangement may be discontinued next month.

Discontinued by the company or by its contractors? In this case the thought needs to be rounded off.

Hook Up Your "Whos" and "Whats"

The classic parody of confused pronouns is the famous skit by the old-time comedians Abbott and Costello, "Who's on First?"

Who's on first?
Yes.
I said, Who's on first?
That's right.
What's the man's name?
What's on second.
Who's on second?
No, he's on first.

And so on. *Who, what, them, they,* and similar pronouns become more ambiguous as they stray farther from the words to which they relate. Take this sentence:

The field people asked that the engineering staff be invited to the meeting because they needed to know more about the new modifications.

Who needs to know more—the field people or the engineers?

There are various ways to fix this defect. Most of them involve moving the related words closer together:

The field people, who needed to know more about the new modifications, asked that the engineering staff be invited to the meeting.

Break It Up

When a sentence looks complicated, break it up.

You can avoid a lot of grammatical traps by applying this rule. And you can avoid awkward constructions as well. "Break it up" is useful in dealing with dangling modifiers like this one:

> The plan to reorganize the Overseas Division, which has been criticized by the Policy Committee . . .

Is it the plan or the division that has been criticized? You can move the modifier closer to the word it modifies:

> The plan, which has been criticized by the Policy Committee, to reorganize the Overseas Division . . .

No improvement. Let's break it up:

> The plan to reorganize the Overseas Division has been criticized by the Policy Committee. This plan . . .

It's good to spot ambiguities within a sentence. It's sometimes bad to try to correct them by juggling the words but trying to keep the commitment to one sentence. Making two or more sentences is a handy way to clarify without awkwardness.

You "Anticipate" It—But Do You Expect It?

"Anticipate" is often used where "expect" would do. In many cases there is no real harm in this usage. "Anticipate" is longer, and maybe it sounds a little more important than "expect."

But anticipate, besides meaning "await as likely," can also mean "act in advance of" or "prevent by acting in advance." So the word may be confusing:

> We anticipated an increase in the price of raw materials.

Does this sentence mean you acted to prevent any bad effects from the price increase—by buying up raw materials in advance? Or does it simply mean that you were not surprised when the price went up?

When you're talking about foreseeing events or developments, use "expect."

The "Effect" Effect

Now and then you come across a usage like this:

One of our primary objectives must be to effect significant changes in our ways of measuring the impact of point-of-purchase advertising.

"Effect," when used like this, is a kind of ballast that makes the sentence longer without giving it more substance. Better to say:

One of our primary objectives must be to change significantly our ways of measuring the effectiveness of point-of -purchase advertising.

There are a lot of nouns that don't work so well when they're turned into verbs. "Effect" is one.

Who Sent This?

A memo arrives on the desks of a number of executives throughout a large company:

To: District Managers
From: Larry Corcoran

To improve our analysis of prospect source documents (PSDs), it is requested that copies of all PSDs be sent to this office for processing, with cover sheets indicating name of field rep, status of account, and projected action.
    Thank you for your cooperation.

The trouble was that nobody had ever heard of Larry Corcoran, nor did anyone have a clear idea of what Mr. Corcoran was going to do with the documents. He was evidently a staff person doing some kind of analysis, but that was about all that could be inferred.

So the request was largely ignored.

When you write to a lot of people—especially when you're asking for their cooperation—assume that at least some of them don't know who you are or why you're writing to them. So explain. Give your position and the reason for the project.

It's Important to Avoid "Importantly"

"Importantly" is not confusing, but it is clumsy:

More importantly, we have instituted a quality control program.

We are achieving quota in calls and sales. More importantly, we're 10 percent ahead of quota in volume.

Sometimes you can just eliminate the "more importantly" modifier. Context makes the importance clear:

We are achieving quota in calls and sales. And we're 10 percent ahead of quota in volume.

Or you can reword:

It's even more important that we have instituted a quality control program.

Sentences with a Split Personality

One good thing about short sentences is that they keep you out of the trap of split sentence structure. When you load too many points—relevant though they may be—between the beginning and end, you wind up with something like this:

In the three test districts, which vary widely in demographics and which have been selected to provide us with results which, when weighted, can be matched against the preset criteria, we plan to convert all distributors to the full-line plan before the end of the second quarter.

Put the working ends of the sentence closer together:

In the three test districts we plan to convert all distributors . . .

Then follow with the other material.

The Denial of "Self"

The specifications will be sent to yourself before . . .
My key people will join myself . . .

"Myself" and "yourself" should not be used merely to avoid using the blunter pronouns "me" and "you." The "self" words (myself, yourself, itself, etc.) are *reflexive* pronouns, used in sentences whose subject and object refer to the same person or thing:

At first he was inclined to exclude himself.

Don't use "self" words instead of a simple *I, you, me.*

When the question arises, remember—*Keep the "self" out of it.* Use the short words. They're the right ones:

The specifications will be sent to you . . .
My key people will join me . . .

When "This" Can't Carry the Load

Your readers should always know exactly where they are as they make their way through the document. It's your job to nail up the required signs. Here's a case where the signpost is confusing:

The Southwestern Region will meet in Atlanta in October to plan a campaign to supplement our highly successful Full-Shelf promotion with a series of new product introductions. This will bring together the efforts of Sales, Merchandising, and Store Relations.

The "this" which starts the second sentence is meant as an indicator, but it's too vague. Does "this" refer to the meeting, the campaign, the promotion?

Help the reader out with a clear sign:

The Southwestern Region will meet in Atlanta in October to plan a campaign to supplement our highly successful Full-Shelf promotion with a series of new product introductions. The combination of Full-Shelf and new product intros will bring together the efforts of Sales, Merchandising, and Store Relations.

"It" Came from Nowhere

It is anticipated . . .
It is recommended . . .
It is suggested . . .
It may be concluded . . .

You weaken your writing when you use "it is" along with the past tense of a verb. Sometimes writers use this phrase because they're squeamish about saying "I." Somehow "I" seems too self-assertive. Another reason for using this weak construction is to edge away from making a direct statement or assertion, especially about an unpopular subject.

Write positively. Say "We anticipate"; "I recommend"; and so on. Your document is stronger, and you emerge as a more decisive personality.

Bullets, Not Blanks

Bullets have impact, especially on a CRT. When you're writing for the screen, it helps to break up blocks of copy into discrete bits.

Bullets are a standard device. However, be careful. Bullet points should be

- similar in form.
- similar in content.
- short.

Look at the following passage:

The communications system we propose

- connects workstations directly.
- will enable us to use various E-mail services to transmit to points outside the office.
- doesn't have conflicting protocols.
- should not be charged against divisional operating budget.

The first bullet point is fine. The second is too long. It's also in a different form from point 1. The third point should be stated positively to match what has gone before.

And the fourth point doesn't belong here at all. The first three relate to the performance of the system. The fourth relates to budget. Locate it elsewhere.

Here's how the revised passage might look:

The communications system we propose

- connects workstations directly.
- gives us E-mail capability.
- eliminates conflicting protocols.

"Screen writing" requires that you break up solid copy whenever it's feasible. Give your bullets impact with consistency and point.

Symmetry Is Strength

Use similar form in expressing similar ideas. When two or more parts of a sentence are comparable in content, the parts should be parallel in structure.

Here's what happens when this principle is violated:

The tasks assigned to the group are the opening of new accounts and to train user personnel on-site.

It ought to read:

The tasks assigned to the group are the opening of new accounts and the training of user personnel on-site.

Writers sometimes abandon parallelism because they think it's monotonous. They try for variety by writing like this:

Previously, the reorganization queries from customers were handled by the sales department, while now the customer relations department is used.

Better to say:

Previously, the reorganization queries from customers were handled by the sales department; now they are handled by the customer relations department.

Consistency of construction is clearer and stronger.

Two-Way Words

A person who does more than one job at the same time is valuable. But a word that seems to be doing two different jobs is confusing:

Applicants who fill out the forms partially slow down the process.

Do the applicants fill out only part of the forms, or do they slow down a part of the process? The sentence could mean either one. Rework it:

Applicants who partially fill out the forms slow down the process.

This treatment is still not great. Revise the sentence further:

When applicants fail to fill out the forms completely, the process slows down.

"Literally" Means Actually, Not Virtually

When "literally" is used to modify a verb, it's often used wrong:

He literally hit the ceiling.
We have literally eliminated competition in this price range.
These cars literally sell themselves.

"Literally" means actually. In the first example the word is used to intensify the fanciful figure of speech. Cut it out:

He hit the ceiling.

In the second example, "literally" means "to a significant extent." The writer doesn't mean that every bit of competition has been rendered nonexistent. Use a word that conveys the meaning:

We have virtually eliminated competition . . .

In the last example, the writer seems dissatisfied with the trite saying "sell themselves." Instead of getting a better wording, the writer reaches out (figuratively, not literally) to grab the reader and say, "I know you've heard this a lot, but these cars are really easy to sell." Use a different modifier:

These cars practically sell themselves.

Keep the Same Person Throughout

Switches from third person (*he, they, it*) to first person (*I, me, we*) or second person (*you*) can be jarring, as in the following:

Phone representatives need to be able to sense when they are losing the prospect. Without this ability, you will lose a lot of sales.

Here's a better way:

As a phone representative you need to be able to sense when you're losing the prospect. Without this ability you will lose a lot of sales.

"We" and "You" Are Us

"You" is usually a welcome word to the reader. But when it's used in directions or instructions, it may be somewhat less welcome.

Contrast the following:

You will be required to be available to work extra time while this campaign is under way.

We will all be required to work extra time while this campaign is under way.

When "you" is specifically limited to the addressee(s), of course, the substitution of "we" is fatuous:

We are assigned as of next Monday to the Kansas City office. Please report there at 9 A.M.

But when the use of "we" can give an inclusive feel to the document, suggesting that "we're all in this together," you may want to use it. Emphasis on the word "you" when handing out assignments and urging effort seems to denote too much distance between the giver of the orders and the receiver.

"It" or "They"

When referring to a group—a department, a division, a company—do you handle it as a unit (singular) or an aggregation of individuals (plural)?

For example:

When General Motors increased prices in midyear, it followed the lead of Ford and Chrysler.

When I visited the assembly department, they were enthusiastic about the new schedule.

Winfield Products markets their low-priced lines under the Hartshorn trademark.

The first sentence is correct. You wouldn't want to substitute "they" for "it"—at least in the United States. In Great Britain "they" is more likely to be used in referring to a number of units acting as a single entity.

The second sentence uses "they" properly. You would not say "it was enthusiastic about the new schedule."

The third sentence sounds a little off. Let's try it another way:

Winfield Products markets its low-priced lines under the Hartshorn trademark.

That's better. When you want the reader to envision several units, use "they." When you want to project the picture of a single entity, use "it."

Always Be Clear about What "It" Refers to

Sometimes when "it" is used to start a sentence, the reference doesn't become clear until later in the sentence:

It is stated in the report that networking technology will render our system obsolescent within five years.

This is a usage that may be all right in conversation ("It says right here that . . .") but not in writing. Start with the word that "it" refers to:

The reports states that networking . . .

Occasionally the indefinite "it" can be used for emphasis:

It is absolutely unacceptable for reps to "batch" daily call reports and send them at the end of the week.

And once in a while you may want to use it for irony or sarcasm:

It seems that the price increase has not received universal approval.

If you don't intend to achieve one of these special effects, replace the indefinite "it" with the word it refers to.

Charts and Graphs—Introduce and Explain

When charts and graphs are included in the document, introduce them by telling what they represent:

Chart 3 shows the relationships among expenditures for advertising and merchandising for the five years 1987–92.

Then follow with brief copy telling what the graphic means:

Expenditures for merchandising have increased significantly relative to advertising.

Graphics usually look crystal-clear to the originator, but they may not be at all clear to the people on the other end. Put in framing copy that explains what they are and tells what (in your opinion) they mean.

Number Charts If You're Going to Refer to Them

If you use just one or two charts in a short document, you should label them, but you don't have to number them. However, if you're using a series of charts, number them, especially if you refer to them in the body copy.

Otherwise, you'll have to use cumbersome descriptions to indicate which charts you're talking about.

The Problem of Sex

"It is convenient to use *his* when both sexes are referred to." This is a quote from the style manual *Words into Type* (Prentice-Hall, 1974, p. 366).

That's not the way it is any more. While it might still be convenient to use masculine pronouns to cover both sexes, the practice is now (at the very least) highly questionable. Wherever possible, *avoid language that seems to have a sexist tilt.*

Some writers complain about this prohibition. (Note that we do not say "bitch" about it.) They chafe under what they feel to be unnecessary and frivolous limitations imposed by feminist ideologues. This writer does not agree. Words have the power to hurt. Language that gives needless offense or pain is unacceptable, even when it is used with the purest of motives.

Given present-day realities, therefore, the sound policy is to avoid potentially gender-offensive words and usages—when they can be avoided without making your writing look artificial or ridiculous.

The biggest hurdle is the gender-specific pronoun:

Each customer makes his choice . . .

Today it has become commonplace to say:

Each customer makes their choice . . .

This usage breaks the rules of grammar. It's jarring; it may offend those who value the traditional usages. Indeed, the use of "their" or "they" in place of "his" or "he" can make you look a bit illiterate. Nevertheless, if the usage seems generally accepted among those to whom you are writing, it may be the best answer.

Another approach:

Each customer makes his or her choice . . .

Correct—but cumbersome and self-conscious. Once in a while it may be all right to use the "he or she" method of avoiding gender-tilt. However, a document that is sprinkled with these combinations is pretty clumsy. Worse, it can give the reader the impression that the writer—for whatever reason—is thinking more about staving off sexism than about conveying a message.

Often the best solution is to shift into the plural:

Customers make their choices . . .

When confronted with a sex dilemma in writing, first try to pluralize. If pluralization would change the sense of what you're writing, use "their" instead of "his" (or the equivalent). It's not pure English—at least not yet—but it's used so often that it works.

Words with "man" in them present another difficulty. "Chairman" is a prevalent example. In some contexts "chairperson" is perfectly good. (The use of "chair" has always bordered on absurdity.)

But the word "chairman" may have a specific connotation, whether the individual referred to is male or female. In the same way, "salesperson" cannot always be substituted for "salesman." In many contexts, "salesman" is a job designation. "Salesperson" may sound more like someone who works behind a counter than someone who calls on customers.

If "chairman" or "salesman" (or "handyman" or any of the other familiar "man" words) is in general use and is established as a handy description, use it. Any attempt to desex the word may be confusing. Even if it's not confusing, it may look affected, diverting the reader's attention from the message. And there are times when such usages can have the effect of actually demeaning women—even though this may be the farthest thing from the writer's mind.

So don't go out of your way to use "man" words, but don't do backbends to avoid them.

There is, however, a whole class of sex-specific words and usages that *are* demeaning or belittling: gal, girl Friday, and so on. Banish these words from your vocabulary. Write "spouses" or "partners" instead of "wives" or "girlfriends" unless the context is so specific that it dictates the designation of gender.

You don't have to be a sexist to slip into the use of language that was once acceptable but is now offensive to some. When there's a commonsense way of avoiding sexist language, use it.

Translating Terms of Art

Experts use a special language that enables them to exchange precise information and advanced concepts. The language, whether you call it jargon or "terms of art," has another value to those who use it. It stamps them as members of a select group. Specialized language is the "secret handshake" of the insider.

When you write to a mixed audience—including your professional peers and those outside the group—you need to compromise. To stick to the jargon leaves out (and perhaps alienates) the outsiders. To write everything in straightforward English makes the document look simplistic to the expert.

Use the terms of art—and illustrate them as you go along. Illustrations or examples are less obtrusive (and far less condescending) than mini-translations or kindergarten explanations.

Here's a good use of the technique from a Western Union document describing a communications system:

> An ASCII file, such as a document created through a word-processing program, or binary file, such as spreadsheet data, can be selected for ultimate transmission. . . . The Address Directory may be thought of as a computerized "little black book" . . .

Twenty years ago, Samuel I. Hayakawa told a group of leaders in management information technology that the most important pieces of information we transmit "are not messages so much as they are metamessages" (*Data Communications and Business Strategy,* edited by John Tarrant, Auerbach Publishers, 1972).

Dr. Hayakawa—the distinguished semanticist who holds the distinction of being the only lexicographer who has been a member of the United States Senate—had come to the meeting to issue a warning. Looking ahead to a day in which a vast amount of business communication would be done electronically, he pictured the dangers implicit in the new way of exchanging thoughts.

Hayakawa drew the distinction between "message" and "metamessage." Two people are talking. One says, "Let's have lunch soon." That can mean, "I really want to get together with you." But it might also mean, "I could not care less whether I see you again or not."

If conversational exchanges were that hard to decipher, we'd often be confused about what people were trying to say to us. But Hayakawa points out that the words are accompanied by other signs that enable us to decode the real message: "a smile on your face, cordiality in your voice, warmth in your handshake." Put these nonverbal components together and you have the "metamessage"—a message *about* the message. In our business and personal lives we send and receive metamessages all the time. We *sense* when a message clashes with the metamessage. A perfunctory metamessage negates the enthusiastic words about lunch. A reinforcing metamessage makes you think, "This person really wants to get together." So you respond with an appropriate message and metamessage.

Hayakawa says, "Sensitivity to metamessage is a function of a power relationship. The more powerful you are, the less you need to understand the metamessage." He gives the example of a secretary who needs to decode the boss's subtle transmissions. As for the boss, he "doesn't need to care how the hell she feels, because he's in a position of superior power."

Here we might part company with Dr. Hayakawa. People in power do need to decipher the metamessages of their subordinates—if they want to remain in power. And they need to use metamessages effectively if they want to communicate with impact.

Metamessages are frequently sent via body language. You have to be within eyeshot to get it. The words the other party is saying are reassuring. But he sits swiveled away from you, not meeting your eyes.

Or the metamessage can be conveyed by tone of voice. You've called the manager of another department to explain that there will be a delay in a project you're working on. She says she understands your problem and can cope with the delay—but her cold, clipped way of speaking sends the metamessage that she is infuriated and resentful—and that you had better do something to mend fences.

When we're dealing with the written word, though, it's harder to send or receive metamessages. Difficulties can arise in a number of ways. For example, disagreement or criticism may be blunter and tougher in print than the author would like it to be because the formatted requirements of business communication don't allow for the nuances that would lighten up the harsh message. It's harder to make a polite evasion in print than in face-to-face conversation—if you're not used to deploying words for this purpose.

It's not that the written word can't be used to convey all shades of meaning. Professional writers do it. And it's not that business writers aren't smart enough or creative enough to send appropriate metamessages in writing. They may be—potentially—very skillful writers, but they have been neither taught nor encouraged to be subtle when composing documents.

The great semanticist Hayakawa, speaking at the dawn of the communications revolution, saw clearly that the written word would become far more important in business exchanges, and that communications would suffer because the metamessage could not be transmitted adroitly or understood clearly.

Today, when more and more business is done through fax and E-mail networked all over the world, the metamessage is as important as ever, but it isn't getting delivered the way it should. Those who are able to write well have a distinct advantage in this environment. They're able to do more than just communicate clearly. They are able to give weights and nuances to their words, convey shades of meaning, enthusiasm, anger, and skepticism, and clothe their messages with the force of personality.

The Thesaurus—A Shopping Mall for Words

"Thesaurus" means treasure, and that's what the book is, a treasure of words. Keep the thesaurus handy, on *your* desk, not out on your secretary's desk. When you're looking for a better word—or even when you suspect that there might be a better word—shop around in the thesaurus. It's a verbal shopping mall, except that you can go instantly to the shop where you're most likely to find what you want.

Get a thesaurus that you find user-friendly. The traditional thesaurus, first published by Peter Mark Roget in 1852, can be unfamiliar and difficult to use. As with most academic treatises, it requires you to look in at least two places—the index and the relevant chapter. The book is organized into categories: space, matter, volition, and so on. When you look up a word in the index, you might be referred to many different categories, because each category treats just one sense of the word. To find out about all the possible uses of the word "soft" you'd find yourself trudging through twenty categories.

Now you can get a thesaurus organized in dictionary form. For most of us this is a lot easier to use. You look up the word, as in a dictionary, and you find synonyms (and antonyms) in a variety of senses. You may also be referred to other words in the book.

A well-thumbed thesaurus helps you find the right word for a specific application. It also provides you with a free shopping spree for words to enrich your vocabulary. Pick it up and browse through it.

Closing Thought

Good writing is the delivery system of intelligence. Your writing should be able to deliver every jolt of voltage your brain can create. If the drop-off between your brain and the reader's brain is too great, you're not doing yourself justice.

Most of the time the ability to write well is not a matter of life or death—although there are exceptions. When Saddam Hussein of Iraq seized American hostages, Mary E. Ewald, of Greenwich, Connecticut, got her son Thomas out by writing an eloquent letter to the Iraqi president (printed in *The New York Times,* September 18, 1990). Ms. Ewald's letter included passages like this: ''I have sent my youngest, well-loved son to work in an Arab country hoping he could help [bring] peace between our cultures. Instead, after 10 days, he was caught up in war. It seems unjust that I, who have given to you so generously, should have my son taken away from me in return. You have the power to right this wrong. . . . I beg you to, in the name of Allah, let my son go.'' Ms. Ewald's letter, beautifully crafted and aimed precisely at its target audience, resulted in the release of her son.

Letter writing doesn't usually lead to fame; but here too there are exceptions. Becky Floyd, a lawyer in Laramie, Wyoming, fumed when a California attorney scorned one of her requests, saying, ''My current retainer is a flat $100,000, with an additional charge of $1,000 per hour.'' Ms. Floyd's response became celebrated in legal circles and made the front page of *The Wall Street Journal*: ''Steve, I've got news—you can't say you charge a $100,000 retainer fee and an additional $1,000 an hour without sounding pretentious. . . . Especially when you're writing to someone in Laramie, Wyoming, where you're considered pretentious if you wear socks to Court. . . . Incidentally, we have advised our client of your hourly rate. She is willing to pay you $1,000 per hour to collect this judgment provided it doesn't take you more than four seconds.''

Computer technology has not made writing less important. Quite the contrary. Electronic communication imposes higher standards of expressiveness and concision. And anyway, words on paper will never go out of style. Paper is handy. You can carry it around, stick it in your briefcase. The computer continues to make inroads, but business communicators will have to shape their messages for screen as well as printed page.

For one things, shaping messages for the computer means writing in ''bites''—short, self-contained passages analogous to the TV sound bite. You may have noted that this book is written in bites.

When you write well, you accomplish more. You look good. You feel good.

And what fun you have!

Don't forget to write—*with style*.

Index